De - Clutter to **FLOW** Better

(application of Theory Of Constraints **(TOC)** in business transformation)

VISWESWARAN SUNDARARAMAN

ISBN 979-8-89363-339-9

Dedication

அன்னையும் பிதாவும் முன்னறி தெய்வம்.

I sincerely dedicate this book to my parents, the living Gods:

Shri. V P Sundararaman and Smt. Seethalakshmi.

Acknowledgements

I sincerely thank the following mentors who have guided me so far in my professional career. What I am today is undoubtedly because of them.

Mr. C Devadoss, Quality, Ashok Leyland Ltd, (Ennore) Chennai, India

Mr. Steve E. Sibley, Director of Information Technology at Watson, Inc. Fort Worth, USA

Mr. Satyashri Mohanty, Co-Founder and Director, Vector consulting group, Mumbai, India

Dr. Eliyahu M Goldratt, Originator, Theory of Constraints (TOC) methodology, Israel

Dedication

To my lovable daughters, Uthra and Hansi,
the best blessings I got from God.

To my lovable wife Mrs. Mathangi Jayaraman, a part and parcel of my life, without whom, I wouldn't have been successful in my consulting career, especially when it demands significant travelling almost every week.

For others, you are my wife; for me, you are my life!

Acknowledgements

I also sincerely thank and acknowledge the support given by my clients and be patient with my consulting stint along the way for the past 28 + years.

Also, a special shoutout to Mr. Bijesh Sankar for his amazing pencil sketches in this book.

Contents

Chapter 1

Get Together

Abhinav rolled down the windows as the car swung into the club's driveway. "Naresh!" he hollered, waving his arms frantically. "Wait up!" A grin spread across his face as he practically leaped out of the vehicle and sprinted toward the entrance, where Naresh—curly-haired and brown-eyed—stood frozen, a twin grin of delight spreading across his own face. The 2 friends hugged each other heartily, patting each other on their backs.

This was the first time they were meeting in person after 5 years. They had survived a grueling MBA course at one of the top colleges in the country together. There were coaching institutes that clocked profits solely from preparing aspirants like them to sit for its notoriously difficult exam. They had met at a local coaching institute, and quickly became best friends. The numerous nights they spent awake together studying, while sipping tea and munching biscuits to crack the entrance exam only deepened their bonds. As luck would have it, they were both placed in the same college, where they discovered the heady fun and rollercoaster ride of hard work and studies of the sort that only an MBA course can bring. Not for nothing do they say that an MBA is a transformative experience. At the end of the 2 years, they were both changed—they were no longer wide-eyed, inexperienced students but trained professionals ready for the challenges ahead. A textile graduate, Naresh had been placed in a company that worked in the same industry—while Abhinav, a mechanical engineer, had been placed in a leading consulting company in the country. Life had taken over then and the 2 friends had hardly had time to check in on the other while they navigated the ups and downs of professional life. It was only now, 5 years later—at a college reunion offsite in Goa—that they were actually seeing each other instead of sending birthday and holiday greetings on WhatsApp.

Abhinav pulled back from the hug. "It's been too long!" he exclaimed. His smile dulled the slightest bit, and a tinge of concern colored his features when he saw his friend's face up close. This was not the Naresh he remembered. Surely his hair was more gray than black? Abhinav remembered how vain Naresh had once been about his hair—he was well-known for grooming himself assiduously, in fact, and Abhinav's own mum had often wistfully voiced her wish that her son would learn a grooming tip or 2 from the Naresh. It had certainly worked while they were in college—Naresh had been the chocolate boy of the batch, universally loved.

No one could resist flashing a smile at him, and they were almost always delighted when they received his trademark wolfish grin in return. Now though—his hair had a troubling number of gray strands, and his eyes looked sunken, with dark circles beneath. Even his smile looked tired.

Abhinav forced his smile back in place. "A drink, then?" he asked. "What else are we to do in Goa?" replied Naresh as the pair walked into the brightly lit club and climbed the stairs to the terrace, which looked out onto the ocean skirting the city's coast. Most of the gang from their batch had already arrived. There, among the mill of excited people, were familiar faces—studious, competitive Jenny, the class topper; Raju, who never seemed to study but still managed to scrape through exams by a whisker; John, the math whiz and now the best market analyst in the country; Priya, imaginative and witty, which made her brilliant at her choice of profession—marketing; Fahad, the CA and MBA grad who was now a veritable shark when it came to mergers and acquisitions. Under normal circumstances, Naresh would be right there in the midst of the crowd, with people hanging onto his every quip and anecdote—he was usually the life and soul of a party. Tonight, however, he lingered near the corners of the terrace, making polite conversation until he seemed to not be able to take the effort anymore. Very soon he drifted to a corner table at a distance from the group, and sank into the chair, looking out at the waves. Abhinav took the chair next to him and pushed a mug of frothy beer to his side, with the élan of an experienced bartender.

Minutes of silence went by while the friends had their drinks as they gazed at the sea. It was a full moon night—the moonlight shimmered upon the undulating waves, and the noise of the sea crashing on the shore was faintly audible.

Abhinav cleared his throat. "So," he began, sounding as cheerful as he could, "How's it going?"

Naresh smiled wanly. "I suppose it could be better." He glanced at the party behind him. Abhinav noticed him looking at Priya, who was giggling and dancing with Fahad. Naresh and Priya had been together at college and were now going steady, remembered Abhinav.

"How are things with you and Priya?"

"Alright, I suppose."

It didn't look alright. If things were fine, she would be here with him now, thought Abhinav. Aloud, he said, "I thought you said you were planning to get married soon."

Naresh hesitated. "I bought a ring."

"And?"

"I haven't asked her yet. Things are—how shall I put it—a bit difficult at the moment."

"Naresh," began Abhinav in a serious tone, "What on earth is going on?"

"Nothing." A smile forced its way onto Naresh's face. "Tell me about yourself. What's been happening? How is consulting treating you? Tell me all about your adventures."

"It's been fantastic, man. I help put companies on the path to sustainable growth—and I tell you, the josh never dulls! My boss is quite experienced in the field, and I've seen some turnarounds that are nothing short of miracles. For instance, one of the companies I worked with was struggling with the age-old conflict of protecting margins versus increasing sales—they found they had to reduce prices to boost sales, while simultaneously realizing that they had to increase prices to boost margins! The firm kept jumping from one side of the conflict to another—it was pure chaos, I tell you."

"Then there was that lighting company—they knew that demand is unpredictable and that in order to protect sales, they need to maintain high inventory to avoid stockouts that lead to sales loss. However, adding more inventory meant adding more cost. When we solved this conflict for them, we helped protect their margins while increasing their sales. The results were phenomenal, Naresh—they achieved an EBIDTA growth of 50% within just 4 months, something that the company had never imagined possible!"

"And then there was another firm that was into EPC—Engineering, Procurement, and Construction—projects. The one truth that everyone agrees on is that projects never finish on time, no matter how much planning is done. The industry is pretty much resigned to this fact, and everyone tries to push everyone else to reduce delays or control expenses. When we started working with this firm, it was on the brink of bankruptcy due to ballooning receivables caused by delayed projects and increasing costs. We were able to significantly reduce the project lead time and yet ensure timely completion. This was a huge value for their customers, and the order book started filling exponentially. There was no going back after that. The company has grown 5 times in topline and 10 times in profit within a span of 5 years!"

Abhinav took a breath. It occurred to him that he had gotten carried away and had been talking for quite a while now. Naresh was gazing at him with a strange, unfamiliar expression on his face. Envy, Abhinav realized with a start.

"What about you, Naresh? What's been keeping you busy?"

Naresh snorted. "What hasn't been keeping me busy?" he muttered. "I don't know how you do it, man—my work is perpetually hectic. I feel like a guinea pig on a wheel that never stops rolling."

Abhinav frowned. "Aren't you a PPC guy at your textile firm?" he asked, remembering that Naresh had studied textile engineering for his graduation. He ought to be having fun swimming in familiar waters, not floundering like a castaway!

"Yes. Production, Planning, Control. That's me. The PPC guy." Naresh paused to take a generous swig of beer. "I joined my textile firm—Pioneer Mills—as a PPC manager. Five years later, I still am a PPC manager. For all you know, I will continue to be the PPC manager when we meet again after another 5 years—if I haven't been fired by then."

"Come on, Naresh…"

"No, listen. I confess I was jealous when you described your job back then. It sounds like you've been successful in your career and I am happy for you, Abhinav, I really am but I can't help but wonder where things went wrong for me. Do you know that Raju has jumped 2 levels since he started working? And he didn't even get placed on campus—he joined work a full year after I did!"

"Forget about Raju. I want to know about you. Tell me about your job." "As the PPC manager, I liaise with sales, marketing, planning, and execution—even with customers sometimes when the need arises—so that I can help plan operations. My role is right beneath the Plant Head, and in terms of responsibility, I sit at the very top. When brickbats fly, I am the first to get hit. It was exciting in the beginning. You know me, I am quite social and love talking to people. But dear lord, when things went south, they went south fast! I feel like I am forever fighting crises. I douse one fire and another one flares up the very next second. I feel trapped, Abhinav. And because I am the sole person responsible for untangling this mess, I feel so alone. I haven't had a win in so long, and my career is stagnating. Come on, even you have to admit that no promotion for 5 whole years is ludicrous." He paused. "Priya… I haven't been able to spend time with her as I used to. I work long hours and even when I am outside the office, this blasted phone does not stop ringing." Naresh looked pained. "She's now heading the marketing division for a unicorn startup. I don't think she quite believes that a mere PPC manager can be busier than her."

Abhinav's heart went out to his best friend. There was more to the story, he knew—the work problems that Naresh was describing were just the tip of the iceberg. It couldn't be pure incompetence—Abhinav refused to believe that and not just out of loyalty to his friend. His gut told him that the issues were simply the symptoms of larger, more serious problems plaguing Naresh's firm. This should be something that he could help Naresh with. He was a consultant, after all—resolving such crises was right up his alley.

Abhinav laid a friendly hand on Naresh's shoulder. "Priya is far too kind to even dream of such a thought," he said firmly. "You didn't notice it because you're still the chump I knew in college—but she's been sneaking glances at you all along, even while dancing with Fahad. That girl, bless her heart, is head over heels in love with you. Now your problem, as I see it, is a rather practical one—we need to fix your situation at work." He suddenly grinned. "Lucky for you, your best friend is a consultant. Let's enjoy the party tonight. I happen to be traveling to Vapi for work next weekend—what say I extend my trip by a couple of days so that you can tell me more about your job?"

Naresh turned around just in time to catch Priya's eye. A heartbeat later, he turned back to Abhinav. "That sounds like a plan," he said, sounding more cheerful than he had all evening.

Chapter 2

A Friend in Need is a Friend Indeed

"Abhi, 2 spoons of sugar, right?" called out Naresh from the kitchen. The pair were at Naresh's flat in Vapi, a cozy little home facing the local park. Abhinav had come over an hour ago, in fact. Naresh was still pottering about the stove making tea because his phone kept ringing without respite. Each time, Naresh would slink off to the balcony to answer it in private. He would return a few minutes later putting on a brave face, but it was clear that he found the calls stressful.

Abhinav was considering making the tea himself when Naresh finally appeared with 2 steaming cups of dum chai and a plateful of Osmania biscuits. "You remember!" cried out Abhinav in delight as he grabbed a cookie. "How could I forget?" replied Naresh as he flopped onto a beanbag nearby. "You hardly ate anything else during semester exams." He groaned as his phone rang shrilly yet again. "I cannot take another call!" he declared through clenched teeth as he silenced the call. "It's a Sunday, for love's sake!"

"I want to know more about the textile sector," said Abhinav suddenly. "You have a bachelor's degree in textiles—teach me, won't you?"

"Alright then." Naresh stretched his legs out onto the floor and got comfortable. "The textile ecosystem is actually quite rich—there are many players, most of whom are small-scale units. Believe it or not, almost all the apparel retailer in the market is produced by roughly 77,000 small-scale units scattered across the country." He smiled, enjoying Abhinav's evident surprise. "Given the fact that the cost of raw materials is ever-increasing, pricing is a key competitive edge to stay in the business. The majority of the textile industry behaves like a commodity business, so not all costs can be passed onto the customer willy-nilly. As for demand, it is significantly influenced by seasonality—Spring/Summer and Autumn/Winter."

Silence prevailed for a couple of moments as Abhinav processed the information. "Does that mean that a company has to come up with new SKUs each season?" he asked presently.

Naresh shook his head. "Not necessarily. There are a sizable number of SKUs—I would say 30%—whose demand is uninfluenced by seasonality."

Abhinav nodded. "Go on."

"Manufacturing lead times are typically long in the textile sector. It isn't uncommon to clock 6-8 months from fiber to fashion, in fact..."

"Wait," cut in Abhinav. "Fiber to fashion—does that mean you manufacture end-to-end products, Naresh?"

"No, no," replied Naresh quickly. "Companies like ours specialize in manufacturing fabrics. Take cotton fabric, for instance. Cotton, of course, is the main raw material we take in as the input, here. But there are many other inputs, too—human labor, machinery, and infrastructural facilities. The process is arguably long and complex. First, the raw cotton needs to be separated from the seeds through an activity called ginning; then the raw is spun into threads through spinning; then it is woven into fabric, which is finally sent to a finishing plant to be dyed and printed. From there, of course, it goes to the manufacturers who use the fabric to make garments that reach the end customers." He paused to sip his tea before continuing. "We consume the lion's share of the lead time, as a matter of fact, almost more than 50%."

Abhinav looked down at the t-shirt he was wearing. "Is that what it takes to manufacture the fabric alone? Four whole months of hard work?" he asked, a tone of newfound respect tinging his voice.

Naresh laughed. "Not exactly, no. The manufacturing lead time in textiles has 2 components—wait-to-process time and process time. The 4-month lead time I mentioned includes both wait-to-process as well as process time."

"Oh. How long does each take, exactly?"

"It's hard to get into specifics, but it's safe to say that wait-to-process time takes longer than process time. In our case, wait-to-process counts for more than 75% of the overall lead time."

"What sort of process do you have in fabric manufacturing, Naresh?" asked Abhinav. "Just the 30,000 feet view, please—not the technical aspects," he added hastily.

Naresh smiled. "As you please. Fiber to fashion manufacturing involves capital-intensive machinery such as dyeing vessels, combing machines, spinning looms, warping & mending machines, and more. Each department makes use of a cluster of machinery, which in turn is managed by individual teams such as Production, Execution, Quality, Material Handling, and so on and so forth."

Abhinav frowned. "But Naresh—if each department is managed on an individual basis, who is the central coordinator that aligns them with the key decisions on what, when, and how much to manufacture?"

"Great question. The central coordinator is none other than the PPC—the role that yours truly plays at my company!" replied Naresh with a dramatic bow.

"It sounds to me like quite an important role!" exclaimed Abhinav, leaning forward interestedly. "Tell me more."

"The PPC horizon begins with Material Planning in coordination with the material suppliers across both domestic and export. It then moves on to Production Planning, which is aligned with the company's market commitments and capacity in accordance with the respective departmental targets." Naresh paused to take a biscuit. "The actual challenge though—that comes when the rubber hits the road. When things don't go per the plan—when priorities shift, when execution changes, when urgent requests rear their heads—how does the PPC accommodate the deviations without compromising the internal and external stakeholders?"

"Oh!" exclaimed Abhinav. "That does sound like an interesting challenge!"

"Interesting yes, but not fun," replied Naresh with a grimace. "It's like walking on a sword's edge."

"Give me an example," urged Abhinav, alert and all ears.

"At the end of the day, any planning exercise, especially in the textile sector, must fix as its prime consideration the maximization of efficiency…"

"Why?" cut in Abhinav. Before Naresh could respond, the answer was on the tip of his own tongue. "Because fabric manufacturing involves capital-intensive machines!"

"Correct. Who wants high-cost machines with low utilization? Only through efficiency can we maximize profits and minimize costs! That's precisely what I seek to achieve, too. I make plans taking into account all the order data available across the board. Sometimes, I add projections from market intelligence into the mix as well. Unfortunately, the plan begins to change almost the very moment it is charted." Naresh arranged the remaining biscuits on the plate to illustrate his point. "Some line items may reach the dispatch section early, while others reach late. Our customers, though—most of them want the complete set of items in accordance with the orders they placed. So the items that reach early must necessarily wait for the rest before they are dispatched."

"Wait," said Abhinav, gesturing at the biscuits. "Why should some items reach early and others late?"

"When individual departments schedule production, they look for ways by which they can increase efficiency—in this case, a measure of productivity. A popular way to do this is to plan large production batches of similar line items—the line managers actually review all open customers and choose line items with similar characteristics."

"Oh! Meaning, the unfortunate line items that do not get batched must now wait their turn."

"Spot on!" said Naresh. "But this cannot be the status quo for a long time - not only would we lose our monthly dispatch target, but we will end up killing customer satisfaction because of the delayed deliveries. So I have no choice but to intervene to expedite the missing line items. I am forced to stop the current production batch that was planned and instead push through a change to produce the missing line items." Naresh pushed the plate away and sighed. "Abhinav, the production department positively detests me. And fair enough, really - these changes weigh heavily on their utilization, which is a prime measure for internal stakeholders. In the meantime, some of the raw material reserves earmarked for specific customer orders - such as yarn, for instance - end up getting utilized for other orders. So I'm fighting fires not just in Production but in Procurement as well. Voilà! I'm enemy number one there too because urgent purchases hurt their cost targets. In the midst of all this mess, work-in-process items and finished goods pile up monstrously. Tell me, Abhi - who on earth would want to keep high stocks on hand in the form of WIP or FG when there is a severe limitation on working capital? And so we end up with tremendous pressure to liquidate these inventories. The piled-up FG is diverted to 'suitable' customers, that is, customers whose orders align with the excess FG stock. The piled-up WIP is then diverted to the processing of other FG orders."

Abhinav scrunched his eyebrows. "That sounds hectic."

A tired smile appeared on Naresh's face. "You would think that would be the end of it, wouldn't you? But there's more. When the customers for whom the stocks had originally been produced follow up with us for their deliveries, it comes as a rude shock to everyone. Where are their goods? Where is the material? Nowhere - they've already been diverted to other customers, haven't they? At the end of the whole cycle, all the company has achieved is a bad impression with both sets of customers."

"Wait," cut in Abhinav. "I get that customers with delayed orders are unhappy. But why should the other customers feel badly done by? Their orders were delivered before time, no? Shouldn't that count for customer delight?"

"Good question," nodded Naresh. "The answer is simple - unreliability. They may have received their orders early this time around, but there's no telling when future orders will be fulfilled. It is quite natural that they're dissatisfied, too."

"Oh!" exclaimed Abhinav. "I do feel sorry for you, Naresh. I feel quite tired listening to you describe this harrowing planning-execution-replanning-expediting cycle - I can't imagine how stressful things must be on a daily basis!"

"Are you still surprised that I'm graying at this age?" quipped Naresh.

"No!" laughed Abhinav. "I think you deserve a chilled beer or 2, old chap."

"Your treat this evening, then!" grinned Naresh.

Chapter 3

The Maze

Abhinav eased his car into his designated parking spot at work. The blue waters of the Arabian Sea shimmered as they caught the Mumbai sun, but their beauty was lost on him. The trip to Vapi still hung heavy on his mind, and he was lost in thought as he rode the elevator. It was only when someone gave his elbow a friendly nudge that he realized he had company. Abhinav looked up to see Gurucharan raising a questioning brow at him.

Gurucharan - or the TOC Guru, as he was more fondly known - was his senior colleague and seasoned consultant with deep experience in the application of Theory Of Constraints (TOC) in thinking and executing management consulting engagements. He had an exceptional track record with the companies he engaged. From his upbeat air, it was clear that he was back in the office from yet another successful conquest.

"What, buddy?" boomed TOC Guru in his usual stentorian voice. "Still thinking about your college reunion, I see!"

"Well, yes and no," replied Abhinav sheepishly. "I met old friends but one, in particular, has a very interesting problem..."

"An interesting problem!"

"Work-related," Abhinav hastened to explain. "Naresh is a PPC manager at a textiles firm and his process seems to be stuck in some sort of vicious loop."

The elevator doors dinged open, and the pair entered the office in step. "Vicious loop, eh?" repeated TOC Guru, scratching his chin. "Come join me for a cup of coffee and tell me the whole story, man."

Abhinav followed him dutifully, launching into a brief explanation as he went along. TOC Guru listened in silence. "And the worst part," exclaimed Abhinav as he came to the end of his tale, "Is that Naresh is a textile graduate! The poor fellow's self-esteem is in shambles. I wish I could help."

TOC Guru calmly sipped his coffee. "Go on, ask!" he said after a while.

Abhinav smiled. TOC Guru had a rather uncanny ability to fathom the unsaid. "Can you help me solve this problem, please?" he asked, voicing the question that TOC Guru had sensed so accurately.

"Done!" declared TOC Guru, abruptly getting to his feet. "I have some backlog to attend to right now, but let's discuss this later today."

Abhinav leaned back in the café chair, feeling a sudden sense of relief. He felt more confident about the matter now that it had TOC Guru's support.

VISION
GOAL 1
GOAL 2
GOAL 3

Abhinav knocked on TOC Guru's cabin door. It was late in the evening, and the office was empty save for a few employees who had stayed back to complete their day's work. TOC Guru opened the door and waved Abhinav toward a chair. His desk was a riot of papers and analysis charts. TOC Guru shuffled through the documents and pulled out a large notepad and pen. "Start," he said, dispensing with the preliminaries.

Abhinav described Naresh's problem, sparing no detail. TOC Guru scribbled on the notepad as he listened, interrupting now and then to clarify a point or 2. At the end of the problem brief, TOC Guru swiveled the notepad in Abhinav's direction.

"Look and tell me what you understand of this," he said.

Abhinav studied the complex diagram on the notepad.

"No?" asked TOC Guru after some time. Abhinav shook his head. He had no idea what the flowchart was or what it represented.

"This, my friend, is a Current Reality Tree," said TOC Guru, tapping the notepad. "A visual, logic-derived representation of the problem described by your friend Naresh. He thinks he's been trying to arrive at a solution through Production Planning and Control processes - but the truth is that he's only been prolonging the issue by managing it."

"Oh," said Abhinav and looked down at the diagram again. "How do I read this Current Reality Tree?" "It's quite simple," said TOC Guru, pointing to the components. "IF (a) Maximizing Output or Profit is the prime measure of every department; and

(b) There is always a bank of orders waiting to be processed; and (c) There are similar line items across all open orders, THEN bigger production batches are formed by combining similar line items across the visible horizon. Like this, each block in the CRT needs to follow the same IF-THEN logic schema," he explained.

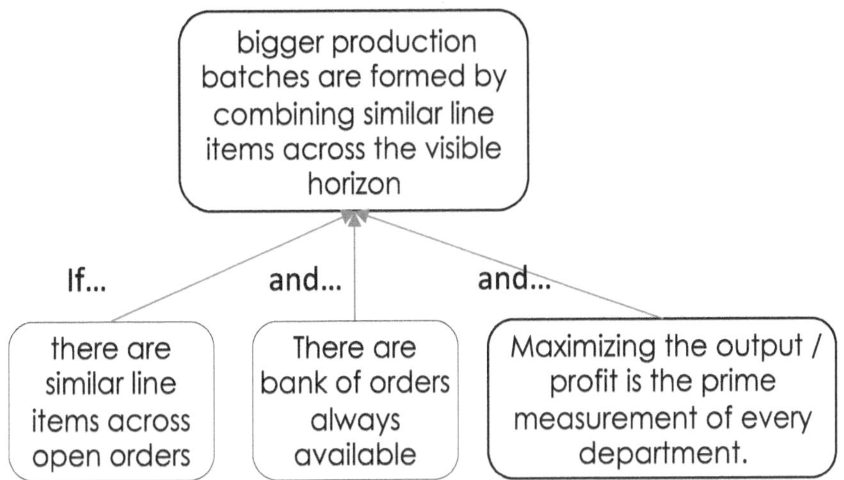

"Let me try," said Abhinav eagerly. "Let's see… IF (a) Bigger production batches are formed by combining similar line items across the visible horizon; *and* (b) What is produced is transferred to the next process, THEN (c) Cherry-picked line items proceed forward," he said slowly.

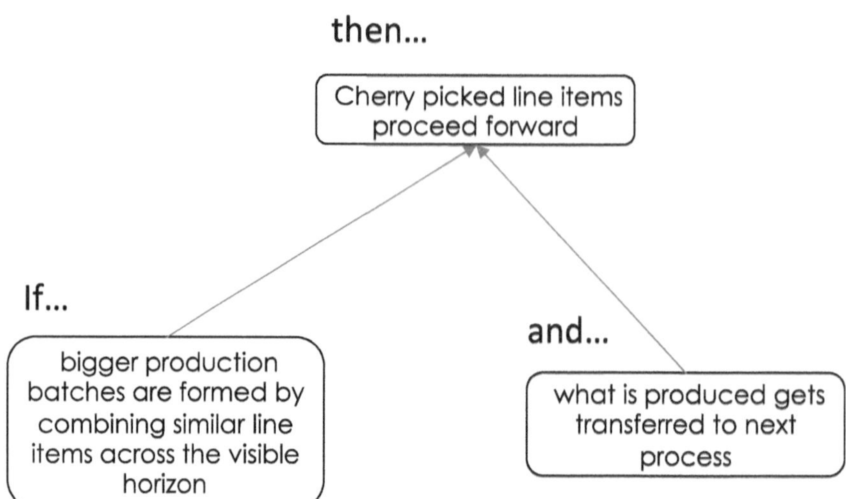

"There you go, man!" cried TOC Guru and clapped Abhinav on his back.

"Wow! This is simple but quite effective!" exclaimed Abhinav. "Well, don't stop there - continue to read the entire CRT!" encouraged TOC Guru.

Abhinav continued further....

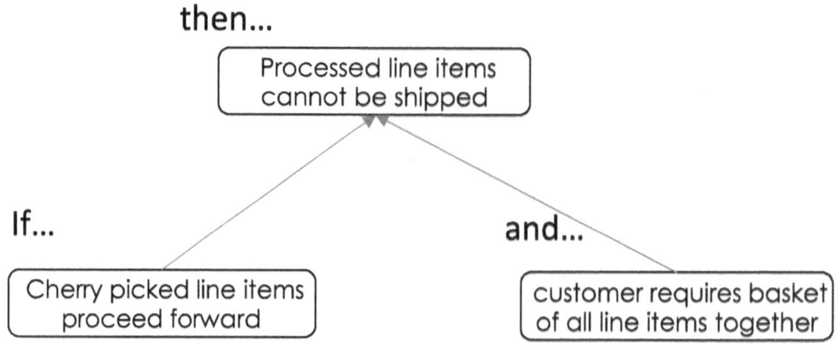

Also, continuing from the other branch of the logical tree, Abhinav continued as

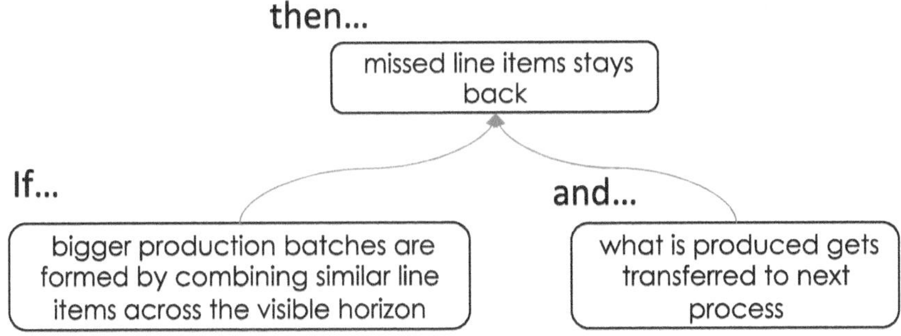

When Abhinav connects these two branches as below, the reasoning behind one of the challenges explained by Naresh becoming clearer.

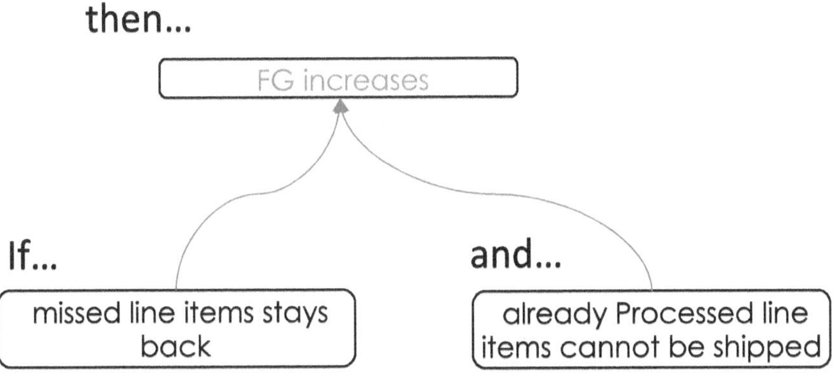

While Abhinav is completing one logical loop, TOC Guru was making corrections on the logical connection to give the final touch for the complete CRT as below.

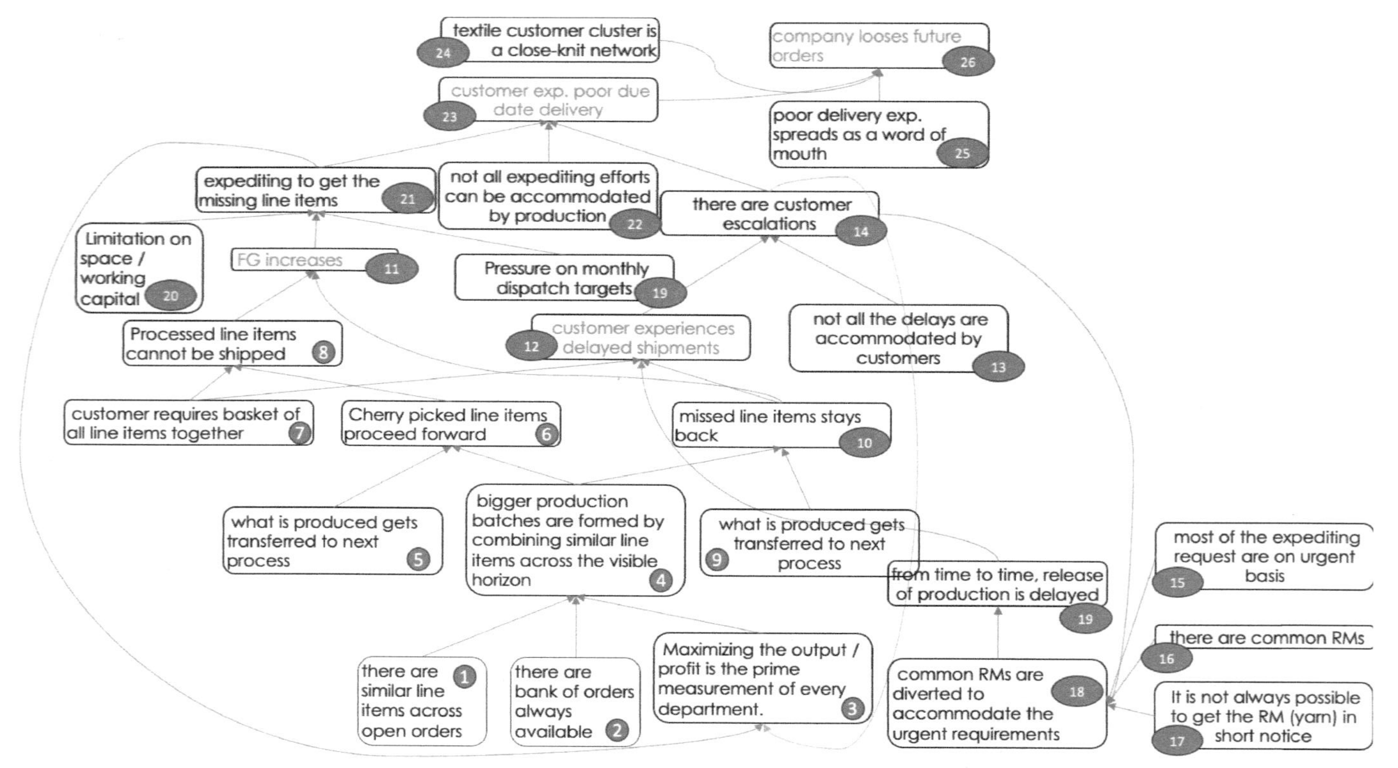

most of the expediting request are on urgent basis
there are common RMs
It is not always possible to get the RM (yarn) in short notice
common RMs are diverted to accommodate the urgent requirements
from time to time, release of production is delayed
not all the delays are accommodated by customers
company looses future orders
poor delivery exp. spreads as a word of mouth
there are customer escalations
missed line items stays back
what is produced gets transferred to next process
Maximizing the output / profit is the prime measurement of every department.
textile customer cluster is a close-knit network
customer exp. poor due date delivery
not all expediting efforts can be accommodated by production
Pressure on monthly dispatch targets
customer experiences delayed shipments
bigger production batches are formed by combining similar line items across the visible horizon
there are bank of orders always available
Cherry picked line items proceed forward
what is produced gets transferred to next process
there are similar line items across open orders
expediting to get the missing line items
FG increases
Processed line items cannot be shipped
customer requires basket of all line items together
Limitation on space / working capital

The final version of the Current Reality Tree they arrived at looked like this:

As Abhinav looked at the final output, comprehension dawned upon him. "I now understand the mess Naresh has gotten himself into!" He looked up at TOC Guru, who was popping a chewing gum into his mouth.

"How do we help him?" asked Abhinav.

"We must understand what governs this Current Reality that is pushing not only your friend but that entire company into a spiral."

"And how do we do that?"

TOC Guru glanced at his watch. "It's past 10 pm, man. If I don't leave for home right now, you will have a couple of angry kids to answer to - it's not a prospect I recommend," he said with a wry smile. He swept up the Current Reality Tree and put it away neatly in a file that he handed over to Abhinav. "Let's connect day after tomorrow. I'll have finished other pending tasks by then - we can chart out a course of action together."

They had spent 3 whole hours in conversation, realized Abhinav. He hadn't noticed the time fly by. "Thank you," he said, with heartfelt gratitude. A problem he thought was a veritable Gordian's Knot had been made startlingly clear and through such a simple process, too! Well, they don't call him the TOC Guru for nothing, thought Abhinav as he made his way to his car.

Chapter 4

The Secret to Understanding the Maze

The next couple of days went by in a blur. Abhinav's work session with the TOC Guru had left a deep impact on him, and he found his thoughts returning to it often. TOC Guru's breakdown of the problem presented a very different perspective from Naresh's account. Abhinav realized that TOC Guru's logical approach - the Current Reality Tree, as he called it - helped clarify his understanding of the core issues at the heart of the matter. It would be immensely useful, thought Abhinav, to learn the technique of converting a tricky problem into a simple and easily understandable diagram. He resolved to resume the discussion with the TOC Guru at the earliest possible opportunity.

It came soon enough. One Wednesday, Abhinav found himself sitting across the table from TOC Guru, who was leaning back in his chair, his hands lazily crossed behind his head. It was after lunch, and Muthu, the office peon, had just brought in coffee and biscuits.

"So, tell me," began TOC Guru as he reached for his coffee, "What happened after our last chat? What's the latest scoop about your friend's problem? Did you get anything done about it at all?"

"Not much," admitted Abhinav. "I want to learn something from you, though. Can you teach me how to convert a problem description into a logical flowchart, like you did the other day?"

"Ah, the Current Reality Tree!" boomed TOC Guru. "There is more than one logical reasoning tool to solve that, you know. The one that I use often is called Deductive Logic, where we deduce the effect based on an indisputable problem premise."

"Ah," replied Abhinav, blinking uncertainly. "I see ..."

TOC Guru frowned. "You plainly do not. Let's take an example, then." He scratched his chin. "Consider this statement. If all dogs have ears and Jimmy is a dog, then Jimmy must have ears. Do you agree?"

Abhinav leaned forward. "Obviously."

TOC Guru threw up his hands in approval. "That is precisely the logic I used to derive the Current Reality Tree from your description of Naresh's problem."

"Oh!" exclaimed Abhinav in sudden understanding. He mentally ran through TOC Guru's exercise the other evening and realized how this simple but effective piece of logic had, in fact, guided the entire session. "So what do we do now, TOC Guru? How do we take this forward?"

"Easy," replied TOC Guru. "As I told you the other day - we must first understand why Naresh and his company choose to continue operating in this logical mess."

"Perhaps they are unaware that they are trapped in a logical mess," offered Abhinav.

TOC Guru shook his head. "I don't think so. This is a conundrum they handle day in and day out, after all. From what you tell me, this is a hellish loop that they tie themselves into every quarter or more likely, every month."

"Oh. Then what do you think is the reason why they continue to operate in this logical mess?"

"There's an unresolved problem underneath this illogical reality. One that I wager they themselves have not understood."

"But TOC Guru, they are well aware of the problems at hand - Naresh told me about all of them, and I explained it to you in some detail as well!" replied Abhinav, taken aback.

"Ah, but Abhinav, all the issues that you mentioned are not problems, not really. They're symptoms." TOC Guru grinned, evidently enjoying Abhinav's surprise. "Dive deep into the symptoms and you will unearth the problem that is governing this logical mess. Once we verbalize the problem and solve it, your friend and his company will extricate themselves from this operational hellhole once and for all."

"Alright," replied Abhinav slowly. "So how do we unearth the problem?"

TOC Guru regarded Abhinav thoughtfully. "Do what I do - discuss the matter in full detail with your friend and a couple of his colleagues."

Abhinav sat up straight. Things were beginning to take shape! "When do we do this?" he asked eagerly.

TOC Guru flicked through his calendar. "Saturday, buddy - works for you? We can take a short day trip to Vapi and meet his colleagues individually and in person. An hour each should do, I think, for us to gain some more understanding about the matter."

"Yes, okay!" replied Abhinav, excited. "I'll check with Naresh and confirm the date right away."

"You owe me, buddy," said TOC Guru, making a face as he sipped his green tea. "Come, get me a nice cup of filter coffee - this green tea will be the death of me. That Muthu's been giving me nothing else ever since my wife had a word with him last month."

Abhinav laughed. "Sure, TOC Guru. I'll throw in a samosa too. Just don't let on that it was me!"

Chapter 5

Deep Dive

Abhinav and TOC Guru were sitting in a small but pleasant office on the outskirts of Vapi, at the textile plant where Naresh worked. The drive had been quite uneventful but slightly longer than usual thanks to TOC Guru's insistence on stopping at nearly every tea stall or dhabha that caught his eye. "The great Indian food trail is the nation's pride, buddy!" he had declared, his eyes gleaming at the sweets and savories that Abhinav suspected were usually off-limits to him. Incredibly, all that indulgence seemed to have had little impact on TOC Guru's appetite. When the receptionist politely asked whether the pair would like anything to drink, TOC Guru sat up so eagerly that Abhinav half expected him to rub his palms together. "We'll both have green tea, please," Abhinav said mischievously, earning a frown from TOC Guru. Thankfully, Naresh walked in at that exact moment.

"Hello, Abhinav! Good morning, Sir - I am Naresh, Abhinav's friend. I believe he's been taking up quite a bit of your time on my account. I hope it hasn't been troublesome, though I must admit that I am grateful - we really are in need of help here," said Naresh, smiling as he shook their hands.

"Not at all - this is our job, after all," replied TOC Guru. "You have an interesting situation here, from what I understand."

"That's putting it lightly," laughed Naresh. "Let me show you around the plant, and then we can discuss the issue in detail. Perhaps you should finish your tea first."

TOC Guru looked dubiously at the green tea. "No, that's alright, I think. Let us be on our way."

"The coffee's better anyway," admitted Naresh to TOC Guru's chagrin, as he held the door open. "The plant's this way - watch your step, please."

The textile plant was not too far away from the office. It was an imposing structure sprawled across 20,000 sq. ft. of land, nearly the size of a small village. Naresh led them up a tiny elevator that opened out onto a steel landing, from where they could see a part of the factory below. Abhinav was stunned at the variety of machinery that the complex housed - there was heavy-duty machinery that each worked on various tasks such as thread winding, bleaching, and dyeing as well as spinning: there were also smaller machinery, such as block-printing and sewing units. The place was abuzz with noise and bustle as people hurriedly worked the machines, pausing now and then to hold urgent conversations with one another.

"Welcome to our humble abode," said Naresh, waving at the scene below. "This unit is responsible for various processes, as you can see. Here, we manufacture thread from raw cotton and weave it into fabric that is then bleached and dyed. Some of the dyed fabric goes on to be printed with designs, too. A portion of this is picked up by wholesale dealers, but we do have clients in the retail space, too - that's what the sewing machines are for.

We manufacture a variety of clothing with the fabric we make, based on the order specifications that retailers and fashion brands place with us."

TOC Guru and Abhinav studied the factory below. Even from a distance, it was apparent that nearly all the workers were stressed. TOC Guru nudged Abhinav and drew his attention to what was clearly a rather heated conversation between 2 of the employees on the floor. A stocky man was waving his arms angrily as he spoke, pointing to the machinery behind him while the bespectacled woman he was arguing with was shaking her head. The irate gentleman suddenly looked up and caught sight of Naresh and began to stride toward them. "Here we go," muttered Naresh under his breath.

"Naresh, Sir!" called out the man as he stomped up the stairs leading to the landing. "Why am I being asked to change the machine set-up for the day? You do realize that it took us 4 hours to prepare this one? Now, I am to bring the plant to a halt to change the set-up again?"

"Ganapatiji, there's been a change in the shipment priority - the Excel Mills order needs to be expedited…"

"The sun was barely over the clouds this morning when I was told that the Clover order was top priority!" exploded Ganapati. He suddenly noticed TOC Guru and Abhinav standing to the side. "Beg your pardon," he said, still surly.

Naresh looked positively relieved at the opportunity to change track. "Ganapatiji, meet Mr. Abhinav and Mr. Gurucharan, or rather TOC Guru. They are consultants who have offered to help us with ways to run this factory better." Naresh turned to TOC Guru and Abhinav. "This is Ganapatiji, the Production manager and a veteran at our firm."

TOC Guru smiled and extended his hand to shake Ganapati's, but the Production manager simply brought his palms together in greeting. "I've been on the floor, helping work the machinery," he explained. "My hands are rather untidy, but I'm happy to meet you both." He turned to Naresh the very next second. "So, it's certain, then? Excel Mills is to be prioritized?" he asked curtly.

"Excel Mills, yes," replied Naresh apologetically.

"Alright, then." Ganapati turned around, and swiftly made his way to the floor, barking orders as he went.

"Don't mistake Ganapatiji," said Naresh turning to TOC Guru and Abhinav. "Truly, there is barely enough time to breathe if we're to successfully pivot the set-up to the new order. He can't afford to stand and chat."

"I like him," said TOC Guru, watching Ganapatiji go about his work with ruthless efficiency. "I would like to have a talk with him when he has some time to spare. Actually," he said, turning to Naresh, "I would like to meet with the teams handling purchase, production, sales, and finance, if it is not an inconvenience, of course."

"None at all. Abhi had appraised me of this requirement, and I've already arranged for one-on-one meetings throughout the day."

Naresh was cut short by the appearance of a rather imposing, mustachioed gentleman. "Naresh Sir," began the man, plainly aggrieved. "Where are we to get the RM to meet the Excel Mills order? Ganapatiji is changing the set-up to put that into production, I hear, but we have only part of the RM, not the entire requirement."

Naresh pressed a palm to his forehead. "Only part of the RM?" he repeated, his voice tight.

"Only part of the RM."

A pause. "Isn't the Olivia order on the same lines as Excel? Can't you divert the RM stocked toward that order?" he asked.

"Olivia is due next week! Excel was supposed to be due only by the end of the month - diverting RM now will delay Olivia and..."

"Let's handle next week when we get to it, shall we?" cut in Naresh tiredly.

Abhinav had never actually seen a mustache bristle with anger, but there it was. "Fine," came the sullen reply, and the man disappeared, presumably to begin the task of diverting the precious RM in time for the new set-up.

Naresh smiled weakly at TOC Guru and Abhinav. "That was..."

"The Vendor Manager," finished TOC Guru.

"Er... yes. Mr. Mathew."

"I think I'd like to talk to him first," said TOC Guru thoughtfully.

TOC Guru and Abhinav found themselves back in the office. TOC Guru had already whipped out his notepad and had his pen at the ready when there was a knock at the door. Mr. Mathew stepped in a moment later, wiping his brow with a white handkerchief. Naresh quickly got to his feet and ushered him to a chair.

"Mathew, thank you so much for taking the time to join us. Please meet Abhinav and TOC Guru, the consultants I told you about earlier this week."

"Pleased to meet you," said Mathew, taking his seat. "I am told that you have a great track record of helping businesses like ours improve efficiency. I was glad to hear it because we could certainly use a hand."

TOC Guru smiled. "Naresh is kind to have told you that, though I won't deny the truth of his account. We have quite some experience working with textile factories, and that is why we are here. I am confident that we can help your situation. We do need your input, though."

"Anything you need."

TOC Guru handed Abhinav the notepad and pen, motioning for him to take notes. "I want to understand your role."

Mathew nodded. "Alright, then. I'm the Vendor Manager and Procurement Head for this plant, which means that I am responsible for sourcing the raw materials to process all the orders. I work with around 150 vendors. The RM I procure is across a large range because this unit takes on various orders from both wholesalers as well as retailers and brands. The vendors I deal with supply everything from raw cotton and yarn to chemical dyes, buttons, and even outsourced jobs such as sewn shirt sleeves. Most are in and around Vapi, but I do have a few vendors that sit overseas." He paused. "I hope I am helping..." said Mathew uncertainly.

"You are," encouraged TOC Guru. "That was a perfect snapshot of your role. Tell me now about the challenges you face."

Mathew sighed, glancing at Naresh. "I'm not blaming anyone here, mind..."

"Of course not," replied TOC Guru earnestly.

"Alright," said Mathew reluctantly. "I think you were there today when we discussed the Excel Mills order? That's pretty much what happens on most days. RM is procured according to the order delivery schedule that we are given, but we might as well be throwing darts at a board blindfolded - that schedule has never been followed to the best of my knowledge."

"What is the departmental goal you are tasked with?" asked TOC Guru suddenly.

"I have 2 vital tasks. Ensure that there is a steady and constant supply of raw materials so that production does not get delayed or stopped altogether. And, I have to procure them at the lowest possible costs. In short, I have to keep both my stakeholders happy – Ganapatiji and Sanjayji."

"That doesn't seem like a very tough task, Mathewji," said TOC Guru. "I have to keep all my clients as well as my management delighted!" He laughed loudly at this, but then quickly put on a serious face and added, "But I am sure there are some complexities here that I am not aware of. Please don't mind this interruption from my side."

Mathew was a little thrown off track by this interjection but continued. "Ah ok. Yes. You see procurement is not an easy task in this industry. I have a few vendors who are quite reliable and who are flexible to meet my varying demands, but they charge a premium. Plus, we will end up having to pay for the transportation of the raw materials too. The vendors won't bear that expense, of course. And, can't really blame them because we do make demands of them at the last minute, and sometimes don't pick up the orders on time. Orders that we had placed, say the previous month. Ganapatiji is not concerned if I have to pay a premium, as long as his department is well-fed. But Sanjay will be after my life if I constantly place my orders with only the premium vendors."

"Hmm. Please one, anger the other! Not a great situation to be in," remarked TOC Guru.

"Anyway, because of this, I often go to more affordable vendors. And, this means, I have to constantly be behind them to ensure that they do not default on their deliveries. Either in terms of on-time delivery or the quality or the completeness of their deliveries. Till they actually deliver the full packet and with acceptable quality, my life is hell."

"But tell me, Mr. Mathew," said TOC Guru. "Can't you and Ganapatiji work this out together? Plan what he needs so that you don't have to make adjustments to your demands?"

"Ha! How often have we tried doing this; but Ganapatiji has his own challenges. I am not entirely sure what they are or whether they really are challenges. You would best ask him directly," Mathew seemed annoyed.

"Sure, not a problem," TOC Guru sensed that this was a long-standing issue between the 2 department heads. He decided to probe another angle instead. "From what you are telling me, it seems you have another important stakeholder as well – the vendors!"

"Oh yes," cried Mathew. "That is a whole new headache. My job description says I have to build long-term, win-win relationships with vendors, of course! Take this Excel order fiasco for instance - with Olivia RM being diverted toward this new set-up, I have been on the phone all morning with 3 different vendors to expedite delivery to ensure RM availability next week. It is a tough negotiation. They may be having orders that they have already finalized, and they would want me to pick those up from them. But right now, that is not important to me, and I try to push them to come up with my new requirements. It all appears futile at times."

Mathew paused for a few seconds, and then continued, "I could pull this one off only because we've been working with these vendors for a long time." Mathew paused again, looking a bit uncomfortable. "Sometimes I have to threaten them. Sometimes I have to ease the leash a bit so that they don't disappear altogether. Don't give them enough business, then these vendors lose all their loyalty. They go chasing bigger fish."

"Raw material availability on the one hand, but cost control and waste reduction are not to be ignored either. Can't put all your eggs in one basket either, and so you have to maintain good relationships with a number of vendors, big and small. Tough job, Mr. Mathew."

"Cost parameters are important. Cannot really blame Sanjay either," admitted a forlorn Mathew. "The textiles industry has cut-throat price competition. Actually, cost control and waste reduction should also be the benefits of building long-term, win-win relationships with vendors. It can't be commercials alone that drive the equation. That's not sustainable. Each week that I get by with the departmental budget is nothing short of a miracle for me. And, things are only getting worse. RM prices are steadily increasing and most of my suppliers have sent revised rate cards. I must admit that I've been forced to stretch beyond my budget to meet RM availability, resulting in outstanding dues. Some of those vendors have choked supply until I meet obligations."

TOC Guru nodded. "This helped a lot, Mr. Mathew. Three crucial stakeholders for you, and not easy for you to keep even one of them happy. Thank you for your time." He turned to

Abhinav. "I think I'll have that coffee now." While Abhinav got up to get a cup of coffee for TOC Guru, Mathew also got up from his chair, shook hands with TOC Guru and Abhinav, nodded in Naresh's direction, and left the room. Naresh took a sip of his coffee and looked at TOC Guru thoughtfully. "Mathew seems excited at the way you articulated his daily struggle. Guess understanding the problem statement clearly is the first step toward a solution, right?" TOC Guru chuckled, stirring his coffee with a spoon that Abhinav had handed him. "Of course, but this is not even the tip of the iceberg, as you can imagine. Miles to go before we even start thinking of a solution, Naresh. Who can we meet now? Will Ganapatiji be free now?"

Ganapatiji was free but did not seem very excited to meet TOC Guru and Abhinav. "I have nothing against the 2 of you, to be frank. But so many consultants have come and prescribed so many things, and I still grapple with my age-old challenges. Don't take it personally, TOC Guru, but I don't think anything is going to be different this time." Naresh was a bit embarrassed to hear this and was about to apologize to his visitors when TOC Guru let out a loud laugh and said, "Ganapatiji, I like your candid opinion, and I don't promise anything. See this as a little bit of a break time and tell us what your responsibilities are and the typical challenges you face on an almost daily basis. Here, have a cup of coffee. I don't need to tell you, this coffee in your plant is fantastic."

Ganapatiji was a little taken aback, and something about the demeanor of TOC Guru seemed to make him relax a bit. He took the cup of coffee that TOC Guru was offering him and leaned back in his chair, making himself comfortable. "See, as the Production Manager, my primary responsibility is to manage production well. I have various departments under my kingdom." The last word was accompanied by air quotes.

"Pray continue, Your Highness," urged TOC Guru with a smile on his face.

"Departments such as dyeing, combing, spinning, warping, mending, and dispatch department, just to name a few." After pausing to take another sip of his coffee, Ganapatiji continued. "While managing all these, I must meet 2 necessary conditions at any time. And these are:"

1) "I must continue to focus on improving my efficiency across all the operations and across all the departments, and-"

2) "I must be able to help my company meet the commitments it has given to my customer."

"Efficiency is absolutely critical for us, as this helps us bring down production cost per unit, and when that happens, profit goes up significantly. And if I am unable to help my company meet its obligations to its customer, not only is my current sales gone, but any future prospects with this customer are in jeopardy as well."

"Agreed, Ganapatiji. But I suspect you are now going to tell me how these 2 goals that you have for your team are pulling you in 2 different directions?" asked TOC Guru.

"Yes, yes," Ganapatiji seemed a bit annoyed at the way TOC Guru had stolen his big moment in coming up with his big reveal, although a trace of admiration seemed to have crept into his tone as well, noticing how quickly TOC Guru was connecting the dots and moving forward in his understanding of the challenges involved in this industry. "If I have to improve efficiency – and I have already told you how critical that is for us – then I have to produce my goods in large batches. I have to set up my machines in order to run my batch. Now, this set-up time is the same whether I run a large batch or a small batch. Obviously, I would prefer to run a large batch, and everybody knows that during the machine set-up time, production is close to zero. And what is really challenging is that batching considerations for each of my departments are different. The dyeing department has its own unique batching consideration, the combing department has a different set of batching consideration, and so on."

"Ganapatiji, can you give us some examples to help us understand this a bit better?"

"Sure, let's take the example of the dyeing department. If I have to produce a batch of yarn in a dark color, then I prefer to continue producing yarn in dark colors as much as possible before I switch to a lighter color. This is to avoid criss-crossing of the colors. So as much as possible, I will avoid or delay taking the light color immediately after the dark color batches. Therefore, what I will do is to go on pulling ahead those orders which require dark colors. I pull them ahead and include them as part of my current batch. If I don't do this, my efficiency goes down. Let's take another example. The spinning department.

There the main consideration is do I need a coarse count or a fine count? So, if I have loaded all my machines to produce fine count, then I look at all the open requests and see if there are fine count requirements for a future date. I pull them ahead and include it as part of my current batch, thereby making it a large one, and which helps me become efficient. Beam length is the consideration in the warping department. Longer beam length requirements will be batched together and once I exhaust those requests, I move to requests for shorter beam length. Almost on a daily basis, I have to plan for such things even though there is a monthly plan that is supposed to help me." And here, Ganapatiji let out a sarcastic laugh.

"Man, I don't envy your job, Ganapatiji. No, not for all the money in the world, or this fine coffee, for that matter!" Abhinav got the hint and got up to make another cup for his senior.

"This is just the tip of the iceberg, TOC Guru," said Ganapatiji. "I am able to do this — producing something in large batches — for 2 or a maximum of 3 weeks in a month. And then, I start getting pushbacks from my internal stakeholders. The sales guys, the logistics guys, etc. Meeting the customer expectations is also important for me and for us as a company."

"What do they ask you to do, Ganapatiji?" asked TOC Guru, while gratefully accepting the cup of coffee that was handed to him by Abhinav.

"Can't really blame them," said Ganapatiji magnanimously. "You see, their customers are pushing them for their orders. A customer might have asked them to come up with 5 line items.

While 3 are available, 2 are not. So, they are not able to meet their delivery targets. The warehouse is full of all the stuff that I have produced, and there is only so much that can be dumped into our warehouses. The sales or the dispatch team need the remaining 2 items before the whole lot can be sent to our customer, but for me to produce those missing 2 items, some input material is required. If he is not able to send me those materials, my productivity goes down. Thus, he will push me to complete those missing line items from all the open orders, forcing me to move away from producing in large batches and focusing on producing goods in small batches!"

Here, Ganapatiji paused, took a sip of his coffee, put his cup down, and continued. "As you have probably guessed by now, the smaller the batch size, the shorter the lead time required to produce the goods. And the shorter the lead time required to transfer them across the departments. And one more 'advantage' of producing in smaller batches is that it automatically increases the availability of machines to produce other orders as well."

"The man is passionate about his work and loves air quotes," thought Abhinav to himself. He was keenly following the conversation and trying to think like his senior.

Ganapatiji was continuing with his narration of his challenges. "So, you see, TOC Guru, by hook or crook, I manage to meet my monthly production targets. During the last week of the month. Like our Thala, Dhoni, who believes that a T 20 IPL match should be won only in the last over of a game." And here, Ganapatiji let out a mirthless laugh. "But unlike our Captain Cool, I don't thrive in such high-pressure scenarios."

"Ah, there ends the similarity between MSD and our dear Ganapatiji," thought TOC Guru, after trying unsuccessfully to picture a long-haired Ganapatiji with a three-day stubble on his chin, walking out onto the plant floor with a cricket bat in hand.

Quickly shaking his head to rid himself of this mental image, TOC Guru said, "Fascinating, Ganapatiji. Let me guess what you are about to say next. Come the first week of the next month, you will again go back to producing in large batches?"

"Yes, TOC Guru. I have no choice in the matter. I need to meet my efficiency targets," exploded Ganapatiji, thumping his hand on the table and stressing the word "need." Abhinav somehow managed to ensure that his empty coffee cup did not fly off the table and crash onto the floor.

Ganapatiji took a sip of water to calm himself down and continued. "This has been my life for the last 2 to 2 and a half decades. Produce in large batches for the first 2 to 3 weeks of every month, and shift to smaller batches during the last one or 2 weeks. And I dread the 31st March, every year." And here, Ganapatiji paused dramatically and looked at the 2 consultants in front of him keenly.

Abhinav understood the cue from Ganapatiji and asked dutifully, "Why, Ganapatiji? Why is 31 March so dreadful for you?"

"Aah, but it is not. Or, rather it should not be. It should be a day of utter happiness for me, but it is not!" Ganapatiji looked very pleased with himself to see a look of bewilderment on the faces of his 2 listeners upon hearing this rather confusing statement from him. Naresh knew what was about to come next and shifted his weight from one leg to the other, wishing that his senior colleague would avoid all this drama and just get on with his narration.

"Very rarely do production managers face such intense pressure on the 31st of March, every year."

"Oh, come on now, Ganapatiji," interjected TOC Guru. "Surely, you are not the only Production Manager in a firm who faces pressure at the end of the fiscal year?"

"I don't know about other production managers in other firms, TOC Guru. All I know is my reality. My annual appraisal happens on the 31st of March. My take-home depends on how well I have met or exceeded my efficiency targets. And the 31st of March is when I was born, born as a father."

And, seeing the look of confusion on Abhinav's face, Ganapatiji felt even more thrilled. "It is my daughter's birthday, Mr. Abhinav. I became a father on that day. Now, for the past 2 and a half decades, I have not been able to celebrate my daughter's birthday, whether it is a working day or a weekend. I am burning the midnight oil reconciling figures, completing other pending tasks, etc. If I don't do that, I can really look forward to being an utter fool on April 1st."

"Ah, now I understand," said Abhinav, thinking that Ganapatiji would have made a fantastic storyteller in some corporate, instead of struggling his whole life being a Production Manager.

"Ah, since one can't move one's daughter's birthday to another day, or son's, for that matter, Ganapatiji, we will have to see how we can make 31st March a day of happiness and relaxation for you. Which it should be, but which is not, but which ought to be," said TOC Guru, mimicking the Production Manager's statement. Naresh turned his face away to hide the smile that was spreading across his face. Ganapatiji was too distraught to realize that he was getting his leg pulled by the visitor. He got up, shook hands with TOC Guru and Abhinav, nodded in Naresh's direction, and took his leave.

TOC Guru got up to stretch his legs, took a sip of water, and asked Naresh. "Who is next? Head of Finance, perhaps? But I need a ten-minute break to recharge myself, please."

"Absolutely, TOC Guru. If you need to use the restroom, please take a left turn and go straight. You will find it on your right-hand side. In the meantime, I will give Mr. Sanjay Malhotra, our Finance Head, a bit of context," said Naresh.

"Splendid," said TOC Guru and proceeded in the direction pointed out by Naresh.

When he re-entered the room, TOC Guru saw a tall bespectacled man waiting for him. What one immediately noticed about Mr. Malhotra was his long, silky-smooth, and wavy white hair. He was also dressed very nattily and seemed to be aware of the impression he made on people. "TOC Guru? Delighted to meet you. I am Sanjay Malhotra, and I manage the finances here," he said smoothly with a smile, extending his hand toward TOC Guru.

"Lovely to meet you, Mr. Malhotra," said TOC Guru, thinking what a sharp contrast this man was from his predecessor.

"Please, Sanjay would do, TOC Guru," said the Finance Head. "I understand that you are here to help us and that you have been talking to a few of our key team members?"

"Yes, Sanjay. Abhinav here won't let me rest in peace until I help him make his friend's life easier," said TOC Guru, pointing toward Naresh while saying this.

"Ah, now I get the connection. Well, whatever be the reason, we sure are glad to have you here with us. Any help that you can offer us will be accepted gladly," said Sanjay.

"I sure hope I can be of help, although your predecessor, Ganapatiji, didn't seem to think anything good will emerge post his conversations with me," said TOC Guru with a loud laugh. "But, be that as it may, let us hear what your responsibilities are and specifically your challenges, as I am broadly aware of a typical Finance Head's role and duties."

"Sure," said Sanjay. "Let me share my dilemma with you. Higher utilization of all our machines, in all our departments — this is my main focus area. Underutilization of these resources is anathema to me and my ilk," said Sanjay warming up. "Underutilization results in an increase in non-performing assets, or NPAs. Lower utilization also results in increased manufacturing costs. And that, in turn, results in lower profitability for our company. Return on Capital Employed (ROCE), as you know, is very critical for me. Another focus area for me would be to lower the operating expenses, but despite everything that one can do to ensure this, some amount of increase in operational spend is inevitable. Increases in salaries to be paid to all employees, increased rents for our buildings to be paid to landlords, electricity bills that keep going up every year although there is no improvement in availability or dependability, etc., etc. I need not spell out such basic facts to you."

After a pause, Sanjay continued. "If I want to maintain high utilization, then I must treat individual departments as profit centers. This is because every department adds to the cost, contributes to the overall cost. And cost as an entity follows the additive rule, as you know. Now, it is very convenient for me to evaluate the performance of individual departments if I treat them as silos. But the real challenge here is – and it seems like a paradox – if I truly desire to ensure high profitability, then I must not treat individual departments as profit centers. Because I do know that like the organs in our body, no department in an organization works in a silo. As a system, they are all interconnected. At the same time, not all the departments have an equal impact on profitability. Some have more impact as they take away much of the time taken in the conversion of invested costs into the market. Or realization of cost into the market value. So that department is more crucial from the value delivery angle rather than from the cost angle. And I really should not be treating both these departments alike; but I have no other option, you see? So, I have always been tossing between these 2 extremes – questioning myself as to whether I should be treating the individual departments as profit centers or NOT treating individual departments as profit centers. And I don't know what the way out is!"

"Hmm. I get your paradox, Sanjay. Thank you for explaining your situation in such a detailed manner. I will get back to you in case I have any additional questions," TOC Guru said smiling. Sanjay got up, shook hands with TOC Guru, nodded in the direction of Naresh and Abhinav, and took his leave.

"Aah, now that leaves us with," and here TOC Guru took a look at his notepad, "the Sales and Marketing Head. Can I talk to him now?"

"Chandra should be free now. I had told him about your visit, TOC Guru," said Naresh while calling Chandra. He spoke briefly and informed his visitors. "He will be with us very soon. Just sending out one email, he said."

TOC Guru got up and stretched his arms and legs a bit, then took a sip of water. "Your plant is in such a calm and quiet area, although all your department heads seem to be quite troubled. We will have to solve this quickly," he said, smiling at Naresh.

"I'm hoping you will be able to help us, TOC Guru," replied Naresh. At that moment, Chandra walked into the room. He was a bespectacled man in his mid-forties with broad shoulders. What one noticed about him right away was his clear brown eyes. He seemed like a man who would not lose his cool even under extreme provocation.

He extended his hand to greet TOC Guru and Abhinav, then settled himself down in a chair in front of the visitors. "Gentlemen, I am at your disposal for the next 30 minutes. I understand you are here to help us, and I will be more than happy to help you help us," he said with an easy smile.

"Fantastic, Mr. Chandra. Please begin by telling us your job responsibilities here," said TOC Guru.

"I am in charge of the sales and marketing function of our company. So, bringing revenue is my key responsibility. Revenue in terms of the top line but also while managing the bottom line. And, my challenge here is rather unique. I have to ensure that the company's short-term objectives are met while also keeping an eye on the long-term goals."

"Can you elaborate on this a bit, Mr. Chandra?" asked TOC Guru.

"Absolutely. My team commits a delivery date to our current customers. Now, this is a sacrosanct commitment. I cannot renege on that. And, I have to do this consistently because that is how our customers start developing trust in us as a brand, as an organization. They will feel that they can depend on us. If I don't deliver as per my committed timelines, their operations get stuck, as you can imagine. And, as the saying goes, once bitten, twice shy. They will go to another vendor or at least start scouting around to see who can be a reliable partner for their business."

"Yes, this is true. And applicable in all businesses. So, why do you say yours is a unique challenge?" agreed TOC Guru but added a question that seemed to bother him.

"Well, I cannot hope to bring in revenue just from my existing customers. It is a highly competitive market out there, and at some point, I will reach a point of saturation with my current share of business. There is very limited scope for expansion with the current set of customers we have. So, I need to acquire new customers, build a rapport with them, and hope to make that relationship a lasting one, while I am still running the current business as usual. I have no choice here – I must have the cake and eat it too, if you see what I mean!"

TOC Guru nodded in agreement. "The man loves his English idioms," he thought to himself with a chuckle. "I see; but please continue."

Chandra took a sip of water and continued. "Another aspect I want to highlight is this. Our current production capacity is not fully utilized. And, I don't know whether Naresh here has told you about this – we have a new, energetic, and dynamic CEO at the helm now. He has ambitious goals to take this company to great heights. He is keen to expand our production capabilities significantly and has already begun moving the pieces to enable this. Very soon, questions will be asked about the utilization of the augmented capacity."

"Very interesting and highly challenging, Mr. Chandra; but good for you and for all of you here if your leader is truly as ambitious and visionary as you say he is. So, what makes you uneasy here? Go and expand your customer base. What holds you back?"

Chandra smiled. "If only it were as easy to do this as you seem to suggest! My challenge here is that for virtually every order currently being executed, I am pulled in. The current shop floor is quite chaotic, and there are misses, quality issues, etc., in almost all the critical orders. Nothing gets done without follow-ups. Not that I am raising any concerns against our dear Production Head, Ganapatiji. I don't know if you have had the chance to talk to him?" he asked, looking quizzically at TOC Guru and Naresh. Naresh nodded his head affirmatively.

"Ah, I see you have met our Ganapatiji. I feel sorry for him, really. It would be really easy for me to pin all my challenges onto him, but then that won't really solve my problems, I know. He really cannot solve all the problems besieging his team. It is clearly beyond his purview."

"That is quite considerate of you, and, if I may say, a very mature way of looking at things, Mr. Chandra; but I still fail to see how this is impacting your abilities to meet your long-term objectives. Can you elaborate on this a bit more?" asked TOC Guru.

"TOC Guru, it is quite simple. I simply don't have the time or energy to look for any new leads. Business as usual is taking all my time. In fact, I barely have time to even manage that. Very soon my ROI is going to look quite dismal, while the CEO is expecting me to improve the revenue significantly. The additional capacity that we are building will come with a cost, as you can imagine! I am expected to grow the business, and new business development is not like a walk in the park. A lot of effort goes in initially, for a small return. It is only over a period of time that these efforts pay off. And, so, I have to start moving in that direction very, very quickly."

"Hmm, I see your challenge now, Mr. Chandra. You have to extend your arm and pluck the mangoes above you while simultaneously ensuring that the towel tucked under your arm does not fall to the ground! Now, now, this is not a native English idiom, but something that I came up with all by myself," TOC Guru chuckled in delight at his own ingenuity. Chandra looked a bit puzzled but got the gist of what TOC Guru meant by this rather peculiar phrase.

"Yes, yes, absolutely. That is my challenge, and I hope you will be able to show me the way forward. This is keeping me up at nights, and I do like a good night's sleep," Chandra said.

"Absolutely. We will ensure you sleep at night, Mr. Chandra. Thank you for your time. We will get back if we have additional questions," TOC Guru concluded the meeting with this remark.

After Chandra took his leave, TOC Guru got up and said, "Now, gentlemen, that was a long day, and I want to get some rest and think through the various points raised by all your department heads. The good thing is none of them is attributing the blame to someone else. They all seem to empathize with each other. That is a good sign. I feel we will be able to turn things around soon."

Naresh nodded in agreement and looked a little hopeful while ushering his 2 visitors out of the conference room.

Chapter 6

Mess Behind the Maze

TOC Guru and Abhinav, meanwhile, made their way to the guest house, which was a short distance away. There was a nice bit of greenery around the building, and the facilities were tastefully decorated, providing a calm and serene environment. Their rooms were adjacent to each other, and as soon as TOC Guru walked into his room, he noted with appreciation the luxurious arrangements inside. The 2 of them decided to have an early evening, and after a light dinner, decided to hit the bed.

"You will, of course, be up by 4?" said Abhinav, knowing TOC Guru's penchant for an early start to his day. "My 'me time,' where I do my best thinking. Yes, of course," said TOC Guru, laughing. "But you can sleep for a while longer. Let's meet for breakfast, say, at 8:30?" Abhinav was happy to get a few more hours of sleep and agreed to TOC Guru's suggestion.

The next day, despite it being a Sunday, TOC Guru was up by 3:30 am, and after making himself a cup of coffee and finishing his ablutions, he set out for a walk around the perimeter of the guest house. The conversations he had with the various departments were fresh in his mind. Each department had its share of frustrations and challenges. No one was happy, TOC Guru realized. He began to imagine the challenges of each department in the form of a conflict diagram – a logical representation of the common objectives of the plant and the necessary conditions to meet them along with the respective actions taken by each department to overcome their challenges which conflicted with the requirements of the other departments.

TOC Guru had worked up a sweat and was feeling energetic after his walk. After returning to his room, he quickly took out his notepad and started scribbling down his thoughts, questions, and pointers as to how to proceed to the next step. After a refreshing shower, he walked toward the dining room, and ordered a cup of masala chai, and started glancing through the newspapers. A few other guests were walking in. The morning was still pleasant, and he could even hear a few birds chirping outside. The masala chai was excellent, and he began to leaf through the menu, noting that the variety on offer was pretty impressive.

"Good Morning, TOC Guru," Abhinav greeted his senior and drew up a chair next to him. "Good Afternoon, Abhinav," chuckled TOC Guru. This was their standing joke, and Abhinav obligingly rolled his eyes in response. "The masala chai is excellent," said TOC Guru when the waiter came to take Abhinav's order. Abhinav placed an order for a pot of masala chai. Very soon, the 2 of them were joined by Naresh who was looking really eager to hear from TOC Guru what his initial thoughts were. "No rest for the wicked, eh?" chuckled TOC Guru. "No, Sir," replied Naresh with a smile. "But I can go a bit later." The 3 of them then spent a few minutes poring over the menu. Naresh noticed that TOC Guru seemed to enjoy a hearty appetite as he ordered quite a few items from the menu.

While the trio waited for their food to be served, the conversation naturally turned to the many discussions TOC Guru and Abhinav had with the Pioneer team. "I have had a few thoughts," began TOC Guru. "There are many conflicts that each department is facing at your plant, Naresh, when I started to analyze them," and here he was interrupted by the waiter who came bearing trays filled with piping hot food. The group waited for the waiter to finish serving them, and then began to talk. "Analyze the conflict? I am not sure I understood that," said Naresh a bit tentatively. "Ah, yes. Of course, you won't know TOC Guru's many mantras. Let me try and explain that to you, Naresh," Abhinav spoke. "And, TOC Guru, please feel free to add or modify as required, of course."

Taking a napkin from the table, Abhinav began to scribble on it. "See, you formulate the conflict using a format like this: 'Because of... we must....'" TOC Guru chuckled, and putting down his fork and knife, took the pen from Abhinav's hand. "The format is 'In order to... we must... because...'" "Oh yeah, I always get a bit confused by the sequence," said Abhinav a bit sheepishly. Naresh was all ears as TOC Guru began elaborating on reading the conflicts.

profit margins are less
we operate in price competitive market

there is a significant price difference among selected group of vendors
other parameters including quality similar across vendors

control cost

buy from low-cost vendors

manage procurement well

there is a premium attached to reliability

ensure RM availability

Buy from reliable vendors

unavailability of RM leads to
production loss cascading to sales loss
lost capacity can never be revived

there is demand unpredictability beyond our control in our business
they can accommodate our urgent or change requests

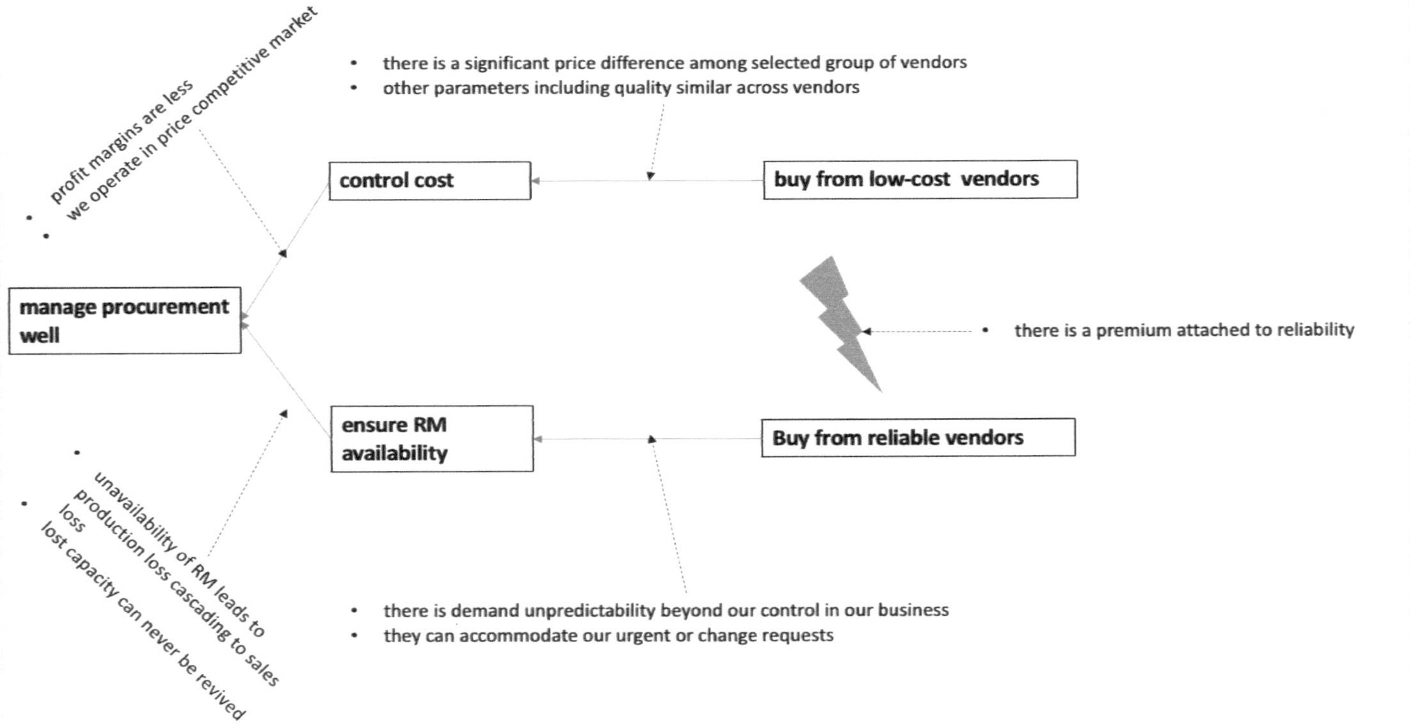

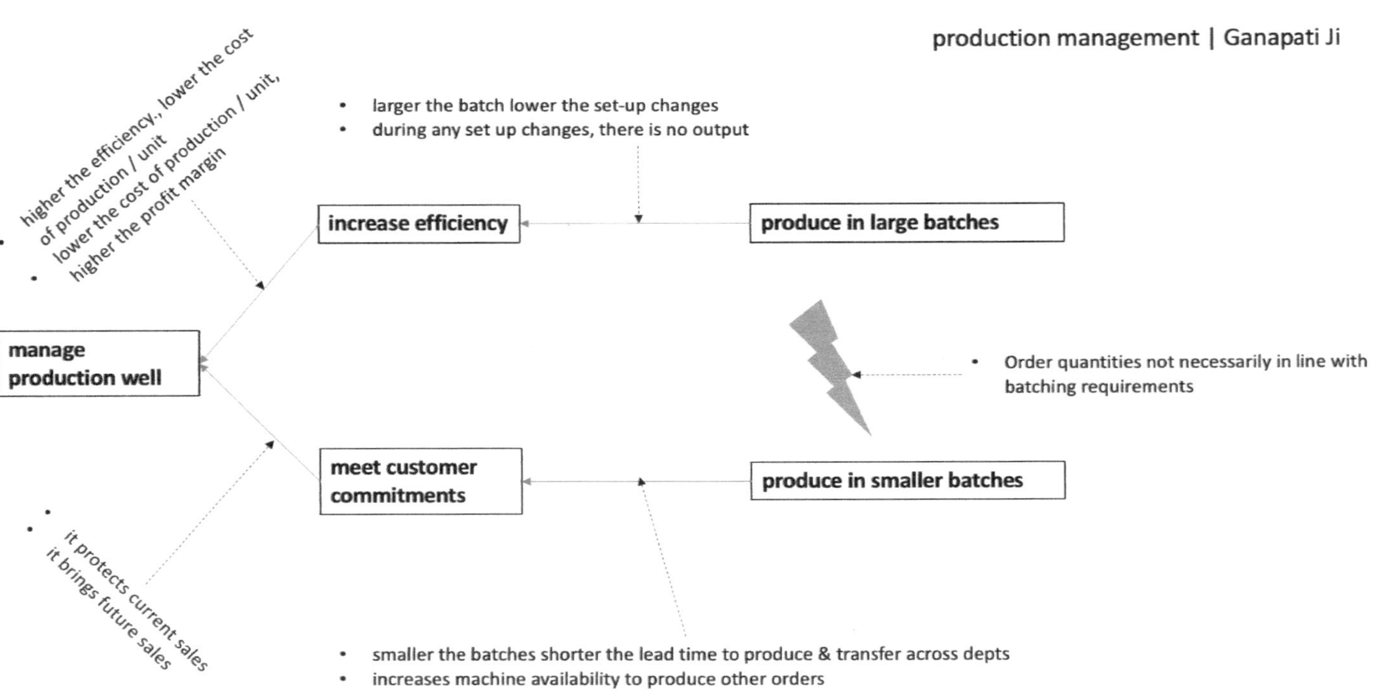

higher the efficiency, lower the cost of production / unit
lower the cost of production / unit, higher the profit margin
larger the batch lower the set-up changes
during any set up changes, there is no output
increase efficiency
produce in large batches
Order quantities not necessarily in line with batching requirements
manage production well
meet customer commitments
produce in smaller batches
it protects current sales
it brings future sales
smaller the batches shorter the lead time to produce & transfer across depts
increases machine availability to produce other orders

Sales management | Chandra

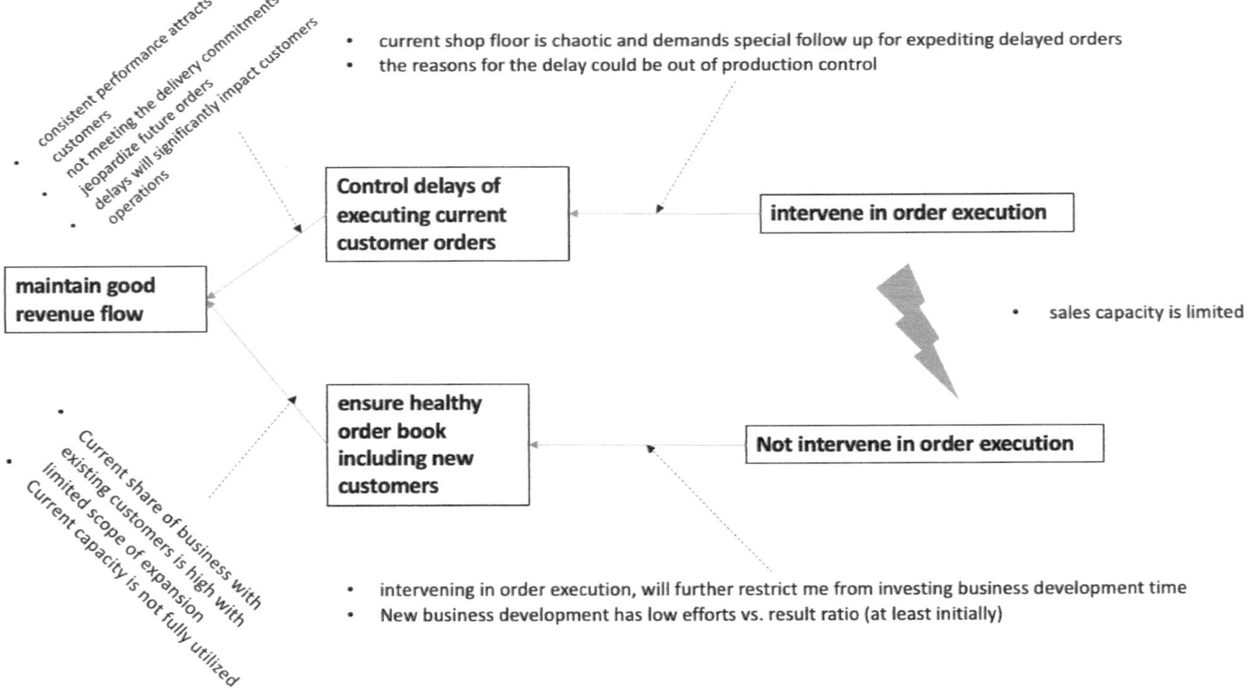

• consistent performance attracts future customers
• not meeting the delivery commitments will jeopardize future orders
• delays will significantly impact customers operations
• current shop floor is chaotic and demands special follow up for expediting delayed orders
• the reasons for the delay could be out of production control
maintain good revenue flow
Control delays of executing current customer orders
intervene in order execution
• sales capacity is limited
ensure healthy order book including new customers
Not intervene in order execution
• Current share of business with existing customers is high with limited scope of expansion
• Current capacity is not fully utilized
• intervening in order execution, will further restrict me from investing business development time
• New business development has low efforts vs. result ratio (at least initially)

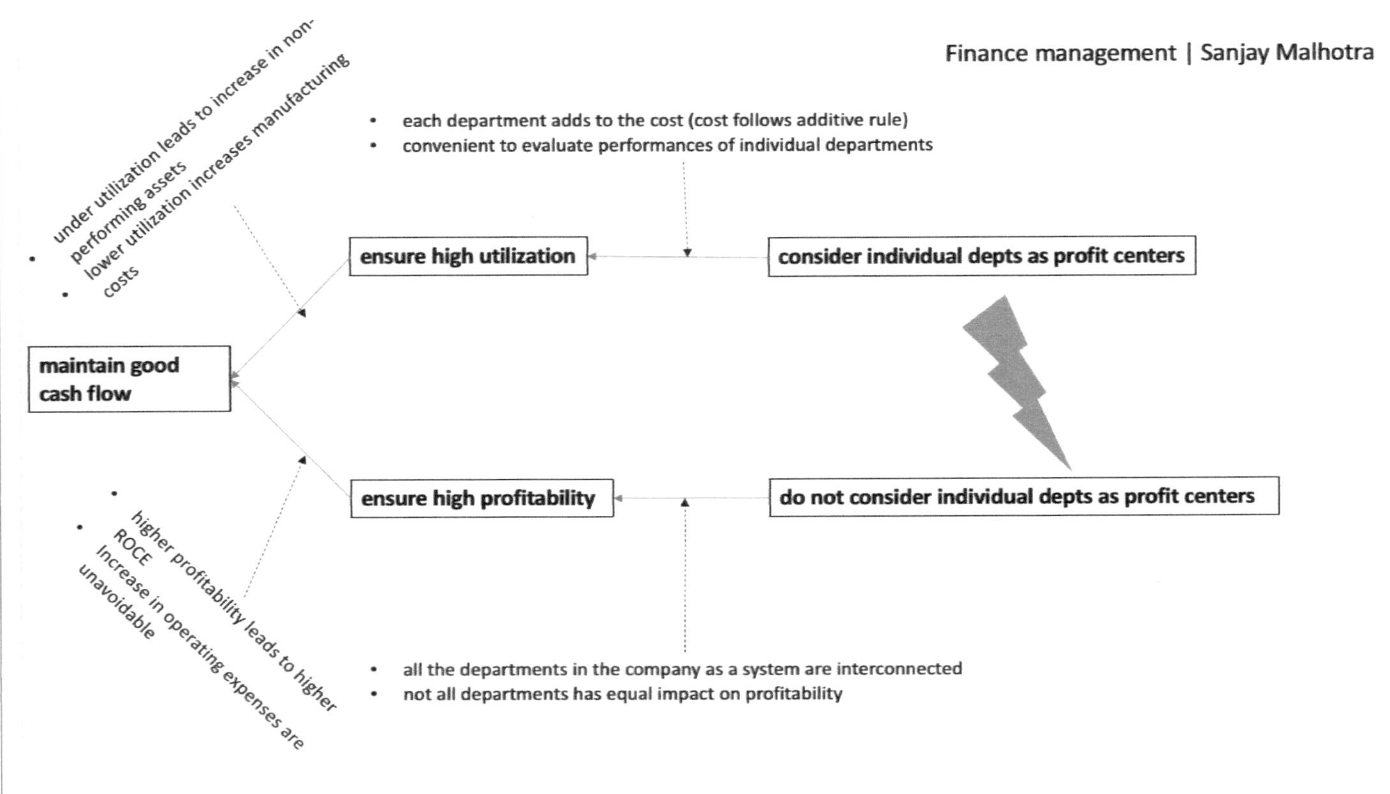
under utilization leads to increase in non-performing assets
lower utilization increases manufacturing costs

each department adds to the cost (cost follows additive rule)
convenient to evaluate performances of individual departments

ensure high utilization

consider individual depts as profit centers

maintain good cash flow

higher profitability leads to higher ROCE
Increase in operating expenses are unavoidable

ensure high profitability

do not consider individual depts as profit centers

all the departments in the company as a system are interconnected
not all departments has equal impact on profitability

He quickly realized that this way of looking into the conflicts was brilliant. "Oh wow, I now begin to see the problems more clearly. So simple, and yet so illuminating." "Yes," agreed TOC Guru, impressed with the speed with which Naresh was joining the dots. "I see that every department is facing some challenges. They are not just passing the buck to me. Hmm."

With a start, they realized that it was almost 10 o'clock. They were the only ones still in the dining room. While Naresh had to go to the plant, TOC Guru was planning to use this opportunity to go and visit his cousin in Valsad. "If she realizes that I came all the way to Vapi and did not go and visit her, that would be my end," TOC Guru told them with a hearty laugh. The 3 of them got up from their chairs and began to make their move to the exit door. "Great start to the day, TOC Guru. How do we proceed from here now?" TOC Guru paused and said thoughtfully. "These individual conflicts … underneath them all, there has to be a core conflict that your organization is suffering from. I am sure of it. These individual conflicts, they are just manifestations of that core problem. But what that core conflict is, I am not sure. I need some more time to mull over this and arrive at the core conflict cloud." Naresh was not sure he understood what cloud TOC Guru was alluding to, but did not say anything, as he realized that TOC Guru was keen to go and meet his cousin. "Of course, please take as much time as you need. I will check with Abhinav, and we can plan our next steps accordingly."

Chapter 7

Simplicity Underneath the Mess

The days flew by, and it was 2 weeks before TOC Guru got some time to think more about Naresh's problems. Being a senior consultant, his time and attention were required in multiple tasks. It was a Friday evening, and a light shower had cooled the temperature. TOC Guru was looking forward to his evening tea and snacks in the office cafeteria. The pakodas on offer tempted him, and he was relishing a bit of the spicy onion pakoda when he saw Abhinav walking in.

"Hello there, buddy. Come enjoy some of these piping hot pakodas," invited TOC Guru. Abhinav was more than happy to join his senior. After ordering a cup of masala chai for himself, he picked up a pakoda and bit into it with great pleasure. "How is your friend, Naresh, doing?" asked TOC Guru. Abhinav told him that Naresh sounded worried and was checking with him if any progress had been made regarding the issues plaguing his company. "The professional challenges are impacting his personal life as well, unfortunately," added Abhinav, sounding concerned about his good friend.

TOC Guru immediately became serious. "Hmm, I can understand that. Compartmentalizing, work-life balance, blah blah blah, are good to show on slide decks. Very, very few people are capable of doing that." Quickly finishing his coffee and snacks, TOC Guru got up on his feet and said, "The weekend starts tomorrow, and I need to go to my farmhouse and take care of a few things. Tell you what, why don't you come along with me? You can breathe in some unpolluted air and not depend on your Alexa to wake you up with birdsong. And I could do with your strong shoulders to get a few things fixed." "Done," said Abhinav, excited to finally see the TOC Guru's famous farmhouse. There was much speculation within the organization about this famed getaway place for the senior consultant. "Where the solutions stare you in the face," as the TOC Guru used to say as he invariably came up with a solution to a knotty issue post a weekend getaway to his farm.

The 2 quickly made plans as to where they would meet and who would drive to the farmhouse, etc. It was decided that the TOC Guru would pick Abhinav up from a spot not too far away from the latter's house. The TOC Guru would bring his brand new SUV, but not being a great enthusiast for driving, Abhinav would take care of that. Abhinav was also charged with bringing a big thermos of strong coffee. "Promises to be a great weekend," thought Abhinav to himself. "A weekend getaway, driving a brand new SUV, enjoying some farm-fresh food, not to mention picking his senior's brains! What more could someone wish for?"

The next day was bright and pleasantly sunny. The smell of rain on the ground was still fresh. "Petrichor," remembered Abhinav with a chuckle as he recalled the vocabulary contests with his good friend Naresh. "Hang in there, buddy," said Abhinav to himself. "If there is someone who can solve your professional challenges, it is this man – the TOC Guru, and this weekend, he is going to really dig deep." Abhinav had noticed the look of sheer determination on his mentor's face the previous evening behind all the banter. He was confident that something major would emerge. With renewed optimism, Abhinav poured fresh, hot coffee into the thermos, shut the lid, and checked once more to ensure that he had everything required for the weekend.

At the appointed time, Abhinav could see a gleaming SUV heading his way, and behind the wheel was a tense-looking TOC Guru. "Can solve the world's manufacturing and production problems, but even early morning traffic is an insurmountable challenge for the famous TOC Guru," thought Abhinav to himself with a chuckle. With an air of sheer relief, TOC Guru handed the key to Abhinav. After loading his bag, Abhinav got behind the driver's wheel, familiarized himself with the vehicle's systems (he knew better than to ask his senior for help here!), adjusted the rear-view mirror, and the 2 set out on their way. The TOC Guru connected his phone to the aux cable. Everyone knew the eclectic mix of songs that the TOC Guru liked. Abhinav was certain that it would be classic Ilaiyaraaja numbers from 80s Tamil movies for the entire journey.

"It will be a good 4 hours, Abhinav. Are you sure you are up to it?" asked TOC Guru, but his facial expression suggested that he was hoping that Abhinav would not say 'No.' "No worries, Sir. I love driving, and this is a dream vehicle. We can stop after a couple of hours, enjoy the view, the coffee, and then move on. Besides, I don't think it will take me 4 hours with this kind of traffic," replied Abhinav, and the TOC Guru looked highly relieved.

As anticipated by Abhinav, the drive did not take them 4 hours. Within 3.5 hours, they could see the dirt road leading up to a sprawling house right in the middle of nowhere. There were a few sheds nearby the house, and one could hear the sounds of cows mooing, while hens strutted around looking really purposeful. A few farmhands saluted them as the vehicle passed them by. As they reached the house, a couple of helpers came out, greeted them, and offered them a tall tumbler of fresh milk. "Ha, so warm and nice," said Abhinav, helping himself to a big gulp. "And, yes, no chemicals," added the TOC Guru. He also directed his helpers regarding the rooms that they would occupy. "Don't worry about the bag, Abhinav. They will help you. Come, let's stretch our legs a bit, and let me show you around."

Abhinav realized that they were not in the middle of nowhere. Behind the TOC Guru's farmhouse, there were a few smaller dwellings, and he could see a power line. "No candlelight dinner then, hopefully," he thought to himself. TOC Guru's farmhouse was not large, but it was built tastefully, allowing one to get the advantages of sunlight, the breeze, etc. The surroundings looked verdant, the recent rains clearing the area of all dust, and the leaves looked as if someone had given them a fresh coat of green paint. Abhinav also noticed a well with a rope and a bucket tied to it. He could also see a few fruit-laden trees, including a jackfruit tree, and a few creepers. The interiors were done tastefully, not luxuriously. There were 3 large bedrooms, all with bathrooms attached to them, and one spacious study. The study contained a large table with a whiteboard in front of it. Stationery was available in plenty, the lighting was just right, and the chairs were just about comfortable. "Just enough creature comforts to let one think deeply. Not fall asleep, Abhinav, my friend. For that, I have a few bedrooms," said TOC Guru, noticing Abhinav's expression and reading it correctly. The kitchen was to the eastern part of the house, and it had all the modern amenities one could wish for. "All organic items here. The cook is a decent chap and can whip up a good, hearty meal for us. Nothing fancy, mind you. For that, you have yours truly, of course!" Abhinav was quite happy to hear this.

"Come, let's freshen up and have a healthy breakfast. Then, we will dive deep into Pioneer Mills' problems," said TOC Guru, looking all charged up. The fresh water from the well seemed to invigorate Abhinav. This was followed by a simple, healthy breakfast consisting of idlis with some freshly prepared curd, some eggs, and a cup of masala chai. "Don't overeat, Abhinav," laughed TOC Guru, putting another idli onto Abhinav's plate.

The 2 then went into the study and sat down to analyze the problem by going over the notes they had made during their visit to Vapi. "We need to understand the core of the problem which is manifesting as different problems experienced by the various teams within Pioneer Mills."

"You mean to say that underlying all the problem statements that we heard from the Finance Head, the Sales Head, the Vendor Manager, etc., there is one fundamental issue?" asked Abhinav. "Is there a method to try and arrive at this core problem?"

"Yes, let's bring the similarities together. The common objectives/needs, actions from among all these conflict clouds in a generic form." And here, the TOC Guru drew a table onto a sheet of paper.

A – Objectives	Department
manage procurement well	Procurement Management
Manage production well	Production
maintain good revenue flow	Sales
maintain good cash flow	Finance
commonality = manage its affairs well now and in the future	

"How can we generalize these diverse needs into one common need? Well, we can do that by stating it this way – Each department needs to manage its affairs well now and in the future. Agreed?" asked TOC Guru. This seemed pretty obvious to Abhinav, who nodded in assent.

"Yes, similarly, when we see some commonalities across other logical entities, the core conflict should emerge. For example, logical link, B," and here TOC Guru drew another table and held it up for Abhinav to see.

B	Department
Control cost	procurement Management
Increase efficiency	Production
Control delays of executing current customer orders	Sales
Ensure high utilization	Finance
commonality = Reduce/ Control Wastes	

"We can go further like this and draw up another set of common objectives across the various departments," said TOC Guru, drawing a third table.

C	Department
Ensure RM availability	procurement Management
Meet customer commitments	Production
Ensure healthy order book	Sales
Ensure high profitability	Finance
commonality = Increase Sales/ Revenues	

"Hmm, interesting," Abhinav exclaimed, seeing how TOC Guru was trying to find the common objectives and needs across individual departments toward a generic theme. "Shall I try communalizing the actions from individual department clouds just as you did for the common needs or objectives, TOC Guru?" he asked excitedly.

"Why not? Go ahead," said TOC Guru, pushing the notepad and the pen toward Abhinav. After thinking about the actions of various departments, Abhinav jotted down his points.

D	Department
Buy from low-cost vendors	procurement Management
Produce in large batches	Production
Intervene in order execution	Sales
Consider individual departments as profit centres	Finance
commonality = Take Actions to Improve Efficiencies	

Abhinav looked eagerly at TOC Guru. "Good attempt, Abhinav," commented TOC Guru. "You can refine the common aspect as 'Take actions to improve efficiencies everywhere, as people work on each and every entity of the organization with a view to improve efficiency — be it their vendors, resources in production, profit centers, and so on,'" clarified TOC Guru. Abhinav nodded in agreement.

He continued to arrive at commonality of actions as below.

D'	Department
Buy from reliable vendors	Procurement Management
Produce in smaller batches	Production
Do not intervene in order execution	Sales
Do not treat individual depts as profit centres.	Finance

Despite multiple attempts, however, Abhinav was not able to arrive at the commonality. Sensing his frustration, TOC Guru decided to extend him some help. "What is the intent behind each of these actions by the various departments within Pioneer

Mills, Abhinav?" he asked his younger colleague. Abhinav paused and thought hard. "I guess the intention of every department is not to let anything get stuck anywhere?" he asked doubtfully.

"Absolutely, young man. And don't sound so hesitant," exclaimed TOC Guru, banging his hand on the table. "Now, think. When do things get stuck?" he asked probing. "When there are obstacles," said Abhinav, and immediately felt a bit foolish. "Fair enough," said TOC Guru encouragingly. "And if you manage to remove those obstacles, what happens?" Abhinav was determined this time to come up with a cogent response and thought hard. "Well, when obstacles are removed, things flow smoothly."

D'	Department
Buy from reliable vendors	Procurement Management
Produce in smaller batches	Production
Do not intervene in order execution	Sales
Do not treat individual depts as profit centres.	Finance
commonality = Taking Actions to Improve Flow	

take actions to improve efficiencies everywhere
reduce waste
take actions to improve Flow
increase sales
manage the company well now & in future

TOC Guru looked pleased with this answer. "Exactly! So, what is each department doing here? The Vendor Management team is focused on buying raw materials from reliable vendors to ensure that they never run out of stock. The production team – well, they want to produce in small batches so that their turnaround time is not significant. And what does the sales team do? They don't want to interfere when the production team is executing their orders, because if they do, the production team's focus is lost. They get pulled in different directions. And last but certainly not least, the finance team does not want to treat each individual department as a profit center. Because even if each department's utilization is high, it does not mean that the system is efficient overall. What then do you see as a common theme here?" TOC Guru posed a deeper question.

"Hmm. They are all taking actions to improve the flow?" suggested Abhinav.

"Absolutely," said TOC Guru once again, banging his hand on the table. "Each department is taking steps to improve the flow. Good, good. Now, can you go and fill the table?"

"We have made good progress, young man. When you fill these commonalities on needs and actions into our cloud template, you will get to know the core problem of this company," exulted TOC Guru. That was a eureka moment, Abhinav felt, reading the core cloud. "What should we do next, TOC Guru?" asked Abhinav.

"Now, we do some physical labor. Your brain has had a workout. Now, I need your muscles to do some work," laughed

TOC Guru, stretching himself. "I need some repair work to be done in the garden. Come, let's digest our breakfast so that Gobindo, my chef, is not disappointed by how little city folks eat! And after that, while you take a nap, you can try to go through the core problem more deeply and see if you can unearth the hidden assumptions behind every logical link."

"Sure, TOC Guru. My brains and brawn are both at your command," replied Abhinav, to the amusement of TOC Guru. "But can you give me some tips on how I can dig deeper into the core issues?"

"Absolutely. For example, try to articulate it this way – 'In order to manage well now and in the future, I must reduce waste, because' ..." Here, TOC Guru indicated a few dots using his hand. "Now, you must be wondering why semantics are important here? The important thing is that these logical connections are called necessity conditions, and hence one must have some grammar to read them. That is of vital importance. Read loudly like this, 'In order to manage well now and in the future, I must reduce waste, because' ... And, you must challenge any assumptions you make and bring to the surface any logical connections you make. Try at least 2 assumptions for every link. And we meet tomorrow morning. I have to go and greet my neighbors here, you see. And help yourself to a tender coconut water or ice apples when you feel thirsty," said TOC Guru with a chuckle.

"Great TOC Guru. Now, let me show you what my muscles are capable of." And the 2 colleagues walked out of the study and strode across to the garden.

Chapter 8

Miss Understood

Naresh was looking at his phone morosely. The way it kept ringing, one wouldn't believe that it was a Sunday. Barely had he finished his breakfast when it started ringing. One call finished and the next one began. "How long can I go on like this?" wondered Naresh. He was supposed to go and meet Priya at a café, and then go over to her house to meet her parents. This was not his first visit, of course; but Priya's father was keen to see his daughter settle down and then actively help him run his company. He was delighted when he had realized that Naresh was in the textile industry as he himself was one of the biggest dealers of multi-brand fabrics. "A PPC son-in-law, and a marketing specialist daughter – what else does a textile man need?" Paddy (as he was known to his friends) was fond of saying this to all his acquaintances.

Naresh got along with his to be father-in-law, although, at times, he found him a tad aggressive and patronizing. He was a self-made man, pragmatic, ambitious, bordering on ruthless. His only daughter, Priya, he doted on, more than his wife. Naresh himself was from a rather middle-class family. His father had retired as an Upper Division Clerk in a nationalized bank, while his mother was a high school teacher. There were no luxuries, but no expense was spared where Naresh or his sister's education was concerned. The family was really proud when Naresh graduated with top honors from a leading engineering college and thereafter from a management institute. Within a few years, Naresh had managed to pay off almost all the loans. His sister also had managed a good position in a leading IT firm in the city and was slated to travel to Germany for a long-term stint with her pharma customer.

"A salary is the bribe that organizations pay you so that you don't leave them," Naresh remembered his friend Abhinav telling him. "Easy for him to say," muttered Naresh to himself as Abhinav came from a rather well-off family and didn't really need to work. His father had made sure of that. The minute he thought that, however, Naresh felt guilty. Abhinav was his best buddy and didn't really behave as if he came from a rich family. In fact, his father had gone out of his way to make sure that Abhinav enjoyed none of the privileges of the rich while he was a student. He took the local train to travel most of the time, didn't sport any fancy phone, watch, gadgets as is the wont of people of that class. In fact, Naresh was quite stunned to hear from a mutual friend how affluent Abhinav's family was. And here he was, genuinely trying to help him out of his situation. Not only that, he had roped in a very senior colleague of his in this mission. "Dr. Watson and Sherlock Holmes," thought Naresh with a chuckle, "trying to unearth the mysterious problems plaguing companies." He was, somehow, reassured after meeting TOC Guru. He seemed and acted a bit eccentric, but that only added to the aura surrounding him. "A hound after his bone, won't give up ever." This lifted Naresh's mood a little, only to be dashed again when the phone rang, telling him that Ganapatiji was yet again unhappy with something.

Naresh somehow managed to calm his senior colleague. His resolution of the issue would be temporary, a band-aid to a deep-rooted malaise within his company. But Naresh didn't know what else he could do, and sadly, he realized, he didn't seem to care either. Whatever had happened to that happy, optimistic, I-shall-fix-the-world's-problems youngster who didn't seem to have enough outlets to expend his energy on? Putting on a shirt and getting ready to go to work seemed like such an effort now. And, this was affecting his relationships. Even his sister was getting concerned. And, Priya? He knew that he was running out of time. No, he was not going to blame her. She had been very patient with him, empathetic, and supportive. "If you are not happy doing this job, just chuck it. Look for something else," she had told him. Naresh remembered how angry he got on hearing this. "Are you trying to imply that I am incapable of managing this? That I am not capable? I am no quitter." Priya had not implied any of these. He realized that within a few hours after that outburst. And in yet another conversation, she had tried to gently reassure him that moving away from the textile industry did not mean that her father would oppose their marriage. "Look, I won't try to sugarcoat things. My father is an ambitious man. He does not intend to give up what he has created painstakingly. Your education profile, your experience, etc., does play a part in him seeing you as his future son-in-law. But that is not the only side that he has. He does not let many people see his other sides, but I know my father. He will be disappointed if he hears that you are planning to do something else, but he will come around. For me. I am sure of that. So, don't let that cloud your thinking. I want you to be happy, and I know that for that to happen you have to be happy in your job."

Priya was right. He was scared that if he moved to a different line of work his future father-in-law would be disappointed. Naresh knew that he had always been the kind of person who put a lot of importance on what others thought of him. He had been going to a counselor for a while now. "You don't owe anything to anyone more than what you owe yourself. Remember that and start thinking about what you need, what you like doing, Naresh." Her words were etched in his mind. But the paradox was, despite all these challenges, he really loved his job, at least, what his job should have been. It was a different matter that he was just not getting to really focus on what he ought to be doing. Fire-fighting was what he was reduced to. "But minus the hero image," thought Naresh wryly. No heroic rescue of a child from the top floor of a building that was in flames. No satisfaction of having done a good job. For Naresh knew that his 'solutions' were never really solutions; they would crop up again the next month. What was adding to his frustrations was the fact that the challenge would not even be any different. Who was that Greek guy who was cursed to roll up a huge boulder up a hill only for it to roll back all the way down as soon as he took it to the top? Sisyphus, he remembered. Some English professor must have taught them in some class. And now, he was living that life.

Determination and stubbornness. What really is the difference between the 2? When does one turn into the other? Quest for truth, beauty versus inability to see the truth staring at your face! Leaders never quit, true. Equally true what Einstein said – 'the definition of insanity is doing the same thing over and over again, but expecting different results!'

Naresh's ruminations were cut short by another phone call. This time it was Priya. "Are you coming or are you stuck in some calls?" Her voice didn't sound angry, only tired. Naresh paused. His instinct was to come up with an excuse as he really was feeling low. The thought of meeting Paddy, hearing his overtly optimistic comments on everything under the sun (despite a recent Cancer treatment he was undergoing) made him wince. But the sight of his friend's photo on the wall – the 2 of them sitting on some beach – arms around each other and enjoying a beer – cheered him a bit. He pictured TOC Guru as Holmes, with a long pipe in his mouth, with that all-too-famous cap of Holmes' – and he suddenly felt a wave of optimism. "This man has seen it all, hasn't he?" He has turned worse things around. Surely, he can help me? And, with Abhinav around to nudge him, if necessary, it was surely a question of 'when' rather than 'if'? "Yes, dear. I will come. Let me take a quick shower, shave and put on some nice clothes. I will be there in a jiffy." Although he couldn't see, he felt Priya get a bit startled by this new optimistic version of Naresh. "Wonderful," she said. "I will place an order for your cappuccino exactly the way you like it, and we shall have that banana walnut muffin that you are crazy about!"

Naresh put the phone down. He felt as if a weight had been taken off his chest. Why exactly he didn't know. Nothing had changed yet; but he felt that it was just around the corner. With a spring in his steps, he went inside to get ready to meet his girlfriend!

Chapter 9

Mess Understood

It was Monday morning, and Abhinav was getting ready to leave for his office when the phone rang. "Good Morning, buddy. How are you? What made you think of me on a Monday morning as opposed to a Saturday night?"

"Oh, wow! I envy him if this is his mood on a Monday morning!" thought Naresh hearing his friend's booming laughter at the other end. He thought of trying and matching his friend's enthusiasm, but gave it up, and instead asked him in his usual voice. "Saturday night or Monday morning – it is all the same for me. Calls and complaints and escalations. Anyway, leave that. Called you to see if you have any updates for me. Weren't you planning to do some deep dive into my organization's issues with TOC Guru? Any progress there?"

"Yes, yes. Was going to call you after reaching office; but good you called. As you know TOC Guru and I spent the weekend at his farmhouse. Lovely place, and great ambience to get some serious thinking done. No wonder that man is so successful. Anyway, coming to your question. You remember that post our discussion with all your department heads, TOC Guru and I created the individual departmental clouds, right? So, the next step was to arrive at a generic cloud for your company. And this we had to do by generalizing the individual clouds."

Abhinav continued to elaborate on the approach, but was interrupted by Naresh. "Abhinav, I am not sure I get what you are saying. Your cloud and the description of your approach are all going way above my head. Can we get into a Zoom meeting or something? And, perhaps you can share some diagrams or documentation with me before that? I can at least go through it once and then connect with you to understand your approach better?"

"Of course. Yes, you are right. It is not easy to get an idea of this without some background. I was planning to leave for the office, but I can quickly tell you what we did. Just give me 10 minutes. And we can connect again on Zoom. How about that?"

The friends agreed to connect in another 10 minutes. Naresh thought what a lucky break it was bumping into his old pal during that reunion. Here is his best buddy actively trying to help him with the help of one of the best consultants in the field!

After connecting through Zoom, Abhinav explained to Naresh how TOC Guru had generalized the individual clouds (objective - needs – actions) and arrived at the generic cloud – as below.

Naresh could now see clearly the common challenge that all the departments in his organization faced, but manifesting in different ways! "Oh wow!" he exclaimed, struck by this revelation. "What next?" he asked eagerly.

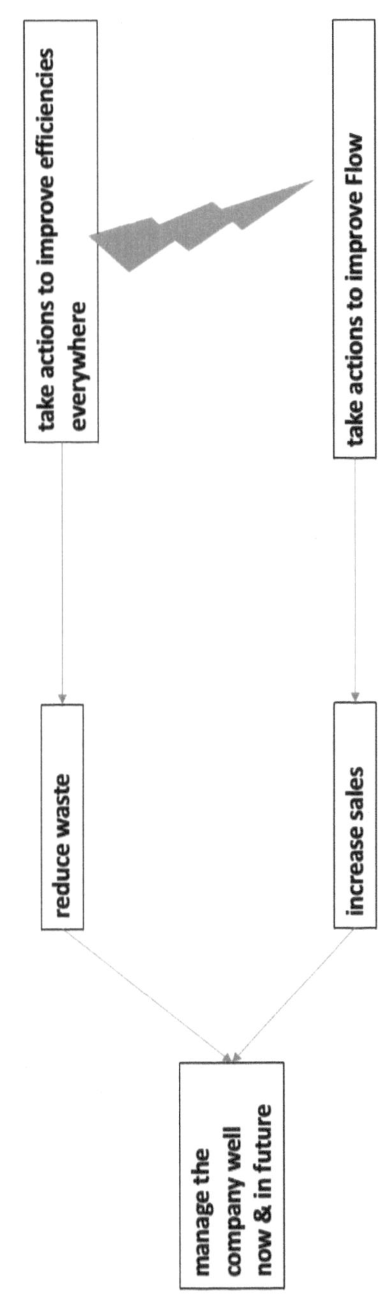

take actions to improve efficiencies everywhere
take actions to improve Flow
reduce waste
increase sales
manage the company well now & in future

"Aah, and that is our homework. TOC Guru does not believe in spoon-feeding," and he let out a big laugh. "He wants me to bring to the surface the assumptions behind these logical links and try to identify the wrong assumption. Somewhere lurking behind all these links is an assumption that appears to be valid but is actually false. We must question each one of them, even if they appear to be very obviously right, true. And that is not going to be easy."

Here he paused, deep in thought. "Tell you what? Why don't we do this together?" Naresh asked eagerly, desirous of being part of this exciting team.

"Absolutely, like old times, eh?" asked Abhinav. "Let's get cracking with this assumption. "In order to manage the company well now as well as in the future, we must reduce waste. Why?"

"Because," Naresh started, but then paused. The question seemed ludicrous. Wasn't it obvious that waste has to be reduced? What is the sense of questioning such an assumption? They struggled to come up with an answer for a while. Then Abhinav had an idea. "Let's stop this now. How about trying to bring to the surface the underlying assumptions from similar links from individual clouds? And, thereafter, we can challenge those assumptions?"

Naresh agreed. Both of them began to go through the links from the individual clouds. And then they got a hint about how they could proceed. "In order to manage the company well now as well as in the future, we must reduce waste." "Why? Because:"

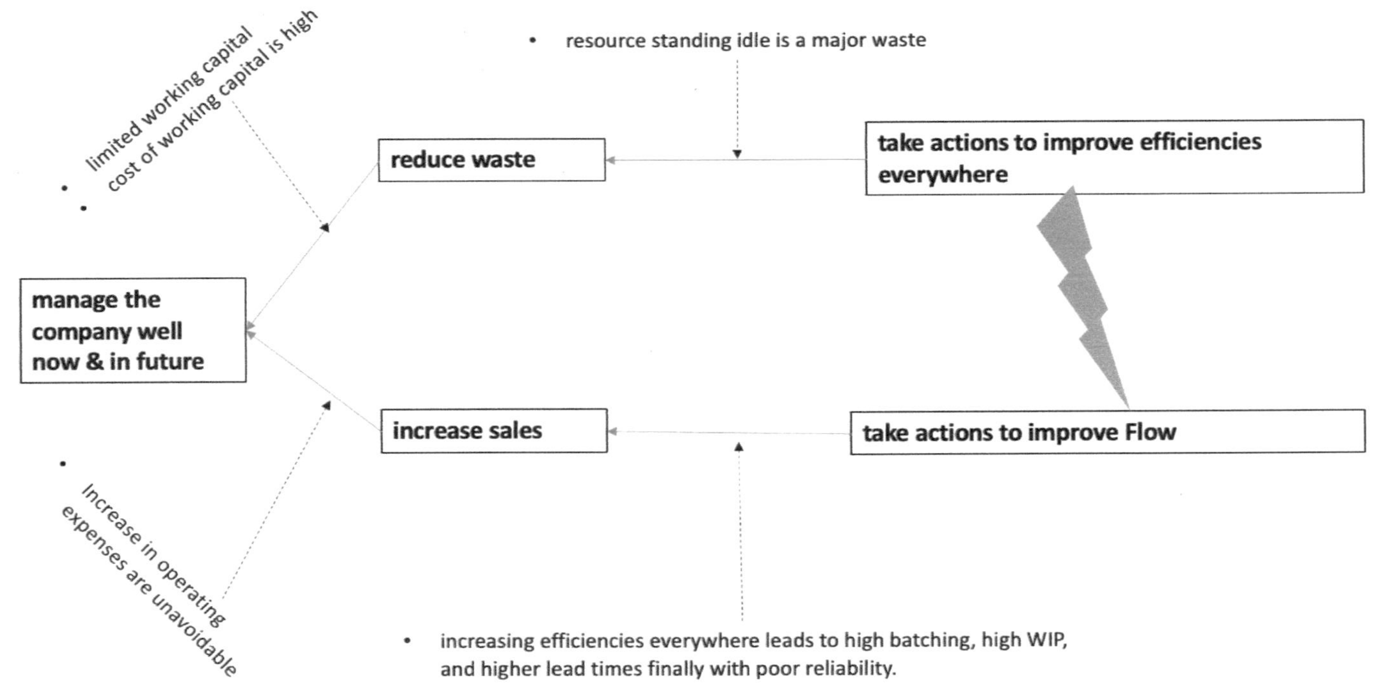
resource standing idle is a major waste
take actions to improve efficiencies everywhere
limited working capital
cost of working capital is high
reduce waste
manage the company well now & in future
increase sales
take actions to improve Flow
Increase in operating expenses are unavoidable
increasing efficiencies everywhere leads to high batching, high WIP, and higher lead times finally with poor reliability.

"The working capital is limited.

The cost of this working capital is high."

They, however, wanted to ensure that they were on the right track, and so the 2 friends re-read the individual clouds and satisfied themselves that the connection and conclusion they had drawn were meaningful.

"Phew! Some progress. Let's get move on to the next one," chimed Naresh.

It was not an easy task — bringing to the surface the assumptions behind all the links. They had to rewrite some of these, challenge each other dispassionately, but the collaboration was fruitful. Finally, they managed to arrive at all the assumptions that could be derived from the generic cloud that TOC Guru and Abhinav had developed on TOC Guru's farm.

"And now comes the difficult bit," said Abhinav with a laugh. He remembered clearly what TOC Guru had told him. Once we bring to light all the underlying assumptions, we should challenge each and every one of them. Check if the connection is logical, infallible. And then, through that process of questioning, identify the wrong assumption to break the connection.

Soon they realized that this task was easier said than done!

"Naresh," Abhinav said tiredly. "I don't think we can do this. This is where the Guru has shown us the way. I admit defeat." Naresh had to agree, for it didn't seem likely that even if they spent another couple of hours pondering over this, they would make any progress. "Agreed. Let's not waste any more of our time. Please take it to TOC Guru. Let me know what he says."

The next couple of days were busy for Abhinav and Naresh. It was Thursday before Abhinav got a chance to catch up with TOC Guru. TOC Guru went through all the assumptions that the 2 friends had come up with. "So far, so good. This seems correct at a first glance. Where did you get stuck?"

"TOC Guru, all this is the easy part, I know, although it took us a good couple of hours to reach this point. You know very well where we got stuck, don't you? Yes, how does one now identify the wrong assumption? All the assumptions seem valid. We tried to find some holes but just couldn't!"

TOC Guru chuckled. "Sorry, could not resist pulling your leg. Yes, that is the difficult part, I accept. It took me a while to master this, I will admit." "You have to apply grammar while you read these assumptions. The way we did before. Just read the assumptions loudly, but this time, add the word 'really,'" TOC Guru said. Abhinav looked skeptical. "Is he serious? This sounds like mumbo-jumbo to me." But he realized from TOC Guru's expression that his mentor was serious.

Almost as if he was saying some incantation, Abhinav started saying loudly, "In order to manage the company well now as well as in the future, we must reduce waste, because, we have limited working capital, and the cost of working capital is high. Really?"

TOC Guru nodded his head in approval and signaled him to continue. Abhinav continued, "In order to manage the company well now as well as in the future, we must increase sales, because, an increase in operating expenses is unavoidable. Really?" He paused to consider the question carefully, and continued.

"In order to reduce waste, we must take actions to improve efficiencies everywhere, because, if resources stand idle, it is a major waste. Really?" TOC Guru looked at him quizzically, but Abhinav continued.

"In order to increase sales, we must not take actions to improve efficiencies everywhere, because, increasing efficiencies everywhere leads to high batching, high WIP, and higher lead times finally with poor reliability. Really?"

TOC Guru asked him to go over these sentences once more. And, this time, while reading like this, Abhinav understood that the logic was not sound enough when the assumption stated that resources standing idle is a major waste. Although he was a novice when it came to the Theory of Constraints, Abhinav was aware that resources were of 2 kinds:

A constraint resource (where the demand is greater than the capacity)

Non-constraint resources (where the demand is lesser than the capacity)

Abhinav paused to ponder the implication of this. "How can that be? Idle time is the devil's workshop as far as factory floor managers are concerned, isn't it? It just can't be true. It flies in the face of all common sense and logic."

"Common sense, yes," said TOC Guru animatedly. "But not logic." He paused. "The logic is not obvious to you yet, and that is why you are flummoxed. Remember what our friend, resident of 221B Baker Street says? When you have eliminated the impossible, whatever remains, however improbable, must be the truth?"

Abhinav gulped. He was still in shock. "So, if this is true," and seeing the look of annoyance on his mentor's face, "and, of course, it has to be true," he added hastily, "the generic cloud gets broken. How do we communicate this to Naresh and team?"

"Are you really worried about the 'how' part here? I would think that your chief worry is whether you will be able to convince them at all about the validity of your conclusion, right?" TOC Guru laughed. Abhinav did not have to answer. His facial expression made it clear that TOC Guru had correctly identified his dilemma.

"Don't worry. You won't have to convince them. I will. We need to taste their excellent coffee one more time, my friend. And, of course, explain to them what we have done so far. Next Saturday works for me. Can you check with your buddy and make arrangements?"

Abhinav looked relieved. "Yes, TOC Guru, of course. I will call Naresh and check with him."

Naresh, it seemed, was waiting for a call from Abhinav for he answered the phone immediately. "Yes, of course. I don't care what other meeting I have that day. I will move all of them to the next week. If TOC Guru is free, that is it. I will make sure everyone else here is free as well."

Abhinav smiled to himself, and confirmed to his mentor that he would indeed have his favorite coffee the coming Saturday. "Splendid," said the mentor and they said goodbye to each other.

Chapter 10

The Myth

Rain clouds hovered over Mumbai that Friday. Naresh looked a bit worried as he peered out of his flat's window. "Wonder if TOC Guru and Abhinav would be able to make it to the VAPI plant. Let me quickly confirm if the rain is going to play spoilsport."

"Are you kidding me?" Abhinav practically shouted when he heard his friend's worried voice over the phone. "You think a drizzle like this is going to deter our bloodhound? He has caught a whiff in the air, and he is going to go after it with all his might. Don't worry, my friend. We should be there at the appointed time. Just make sure all your department heads are there."

Naresh was relieved to hear this and carried on with his responsibilities at the plant with more than usual optimism. He visited the VAPI plant on a Friday afternoon. Finishing off a light lunch, he made sure that all the department heads were made aware of the TOC Guru's visit. He also ensured that there was a good supply of coffee in the meeting room where his visitors were going to be seated. A few minutes after 2 pm, he could see TOC Guru and Abhinav walking in through the door and signing the visitors' register.

"Good Afternoon, TOC Guru," said Naresh, warmly embracing his pal. "Hope the rain did not make the drive difficult?"

"Nothing that your excellent coffee can't take care of, Naresh. That alone is worth the trip, but, of course, your challenges here in your organization are a good puzzle for me to try and solve. In the process, show my promising junior colleague how one should go about analyzing such issues."

With that, TOC Guru took out his laptop and connected it to the projector. The PowerPoint deck was to the point. Naresh and his team were fully immersed in the points that TOC Guru explained expertly. He summarized the key points from his previous discussions with Mr. Mathew, the Procurement Manager; Ganapatiji, the Production Manager; Mr. Chandra, the Sales Manager; and Mr. Sanjay, Finance Manager. Abhinav then took over and explained each and every cloud in a typical syntax:

"In order to …, We must … Because …"

Naresh quickly got the hang of this. He joined his friend in reading the department clouds using the same syntax. However, it was not enough to just document the clouds this way. They needed to get buy-in from the respective department heads. This resulted in a few back-and-forth discussions. But finally, after some passionate discussion close to an hour, agreement could be reached.

"So far, so good," chuckled TOC Guru, getting up from his chair and helping himself to his second cup of coffee. "And now comes the difficult part," he said, letting out a loud laugh.

"Gentlemen, let me ask all of you a very simple question. What should we do now?"

Ganapatiji seemed a bit annoyed by the drama that TOC Guru was creating. "Isn't that obvious? We should proceed to solve each and everyone's conflicts, of course."

The other department heads nodded in agreement.

"Dare I say that that is not the answer I was hoping for, Ganapatiji?" said TOC Guru. He continued, "And the reason for that is this view will emerge when we indulge in divergence thinking. Meaning, when we look at these various entities as separate, in silos. As if all your departments are disconnected." He paused to take a sip of his coffee, and then continued, "But all of you here – seasoned leaders, industry veterans – are aware that all of your departments are interconnected, right? Similar to the various organs in our body interconnected through blood vessels and nerves." TOC Guru scanned the audience in front of him. Quite a few nods could be seen.

"Let us take an example." If procurement purchases materials from low-cost vendors to save money, it is highly likely to lead to quality issues. Say, in the spinning phase." Ganapatiji looked pleased and cast a disapproving look at Mr. Mathew. TOC Guru smiled to himself as he noticed this. He proceeded smoothly. "And, if Ganapatiji decides to produce RM in large batches to enhance efficiency, the Sales Head will have to deal with complaints from unhappy customers due to delayed deliveries." Chandra, the Sales Head, appeared satisfied while Ganapatiji scowled at no one in particular.

"TOC Guru is having a ball," thought Naresh to himself. He quickly intervened. "Point taken, TOC Guru." "All our departments are interconnected through information and material flows."

"Exactly," continued the TOC Guru. "I too saw a common thread among the individual clouds." The audience became curious about what the TOC Guru was going to reveal next.

TOC Guru cleared his throat and started reading out the core conflict cloud using the same syntax as before. He read it out, enunciating each word slowly and steadily, modulating his voice to suit the text, and pausing at each pause to enable his audience to comprehend the logic behind the statements. It took him around 20 minutes to complete reading the core cloud. He clarified a few queries raised by his audience with practiced ease. But that time was well-spent, as the audience now has a complete understanding of the core cloud. There was a consensus among all of them on this topic.

Chandra, the Head of Sales and Marketing, chimed in. "TOC Guru, this is exactly the problem that I have been suffering from all these years." "How do we come out of it, though?" Abhinav was quick to reply, "By invalidating the assumptions."

"By what?" I am afraid I don't follow you there. "Can you please elaborate?" requested Mr. Chandra.

"Absolutely." Assumptions are what hold the link. The underlying truth behind the syntax of "In order to... we must..." is that if any of these assumptions is found to be incorrect, then that specific link becomes invalid. TOC Guru came to the rescue of his younger colleague.

Naresh responded to this explanation. "If I understood you correctly, TOC Guru, it is somewhat like this." And let me try to come up with an example." Here, he paused for a few seconds to collect his thoughts and quickly added. "For example, is it like this?" "I must go to my daughter's school next Monday because there is a parent-teacher meeting scheduled, and attendance by both parents is mandatory."

"Bingo," exulted the TOC Guru. "When and how does this assumption become invalid?"

Ganapatiji, who had been quiet for a while, remarked. "If the school clarifies that it is not mandatory for both parents to attend the PTM, and that it is enough if at least one parent or a legal guardian attends it, then Naresh need not use that as an excuse to skip work and go to his daughter's school whenever he wants."

There were a few laughs around the room as soon as Ganapatiji finished speaking.

"Excellent going, gentlemen," said TOC Guru, drawing the attention of everyone back around to the problem at hand. "In effect, what we have just agreed upon is this: The key to resolving the core conflict is by:

- Exposing all the assumptions

- Identifying the wrong assumptions by invalidating them"

The department heads were keen to try and do this on their own. Naresh noted the excitement in his team and felt hopeful.

A team that works together to solve a common problem is bound to find one sooner than later!

They read each and every link loudly using the syntax taught by TOC Guru. TOC Guru watched them with a twinkle in his eye. He signaled his younger colleague to come out of the room and conferred with him for a while, then came back and settled himself down with another cup of coffee. After 15 minutes had elapsed, however, the group seemed a bit puzzled. Ganapatiji looked deflated. Mathew spoke up.

"I don't think we have made any wrong assumptions, TOC Guru. We have looked at it from all possible perspectives and challenged all our assumptions. The core cloud cannot be solved, it appears. I hope we are all wrong somehow, but right now, I cannot see how that could be the case."

Abhinav looked at his more experienced colleague with admiration. This is exactly what he had predicted when he signaled Abhinav to come out of the conference room a little earlier. TOC Guru smiled at them and said, "If you all agree, shall I attempt to identify the wrong assumption?"

"Of course," Naresh replied eagerly. The group settled down to see how TOC Guru would go about doing this.

Once again, TOC Guru read the entire core cloud using the now-familiar syntax. But when he read the link, "in order to reduce waste, we must take actions to improve efficiencies everywhere, because a resource standing idle is a major waste," he paused. "Gentlemen, is this assumption really true? And is it true at all times? Can't you think of at least one instance when this assumption does not hold water?"

Ganapatiji waved his head as if to suggest that this was a truth that did not require any deep contemplation. There was an uncomfortable silence in the room. Abhinav noted that the silence did not faze TOC Guru. He made no attempt to break the silence but instead allowed the group to continue to think. After a good 3 or 4 minutes, Sanjay, the Finance Head, cleared his throat and began to speak very tentatively.

"I am not sure if what I am about to say is applicable in our case, but here is what I think. I have come across situations where it is not necessary that a resource that is standing idle is a major waste."

"Ridiculous," blustered Ganapatiji. "Just because someone with a fancy reputation comes here and plants this preposterous idea in our minds does not mean that we swallow that without any thought. Sanjayji, are you suggesting that there can be situations, or even one instance where a resource that has been procured at some cost just takes up space most of the time but is not utilized fully, is not a total waste? Come on, don't be so gullible!" Naresh looked at TOC Guru in alarm. Here was someone who was an expert in tackling such problems spending his time and energy trying to help him and his company out, that too, without asking for anything in return except for a few cups of coffee, and one of his own team members was behaving in a downright hostile manner. However, to his surprise, he found that TOC Guru not only seemed least bothered by this outburst but rather seemed to be enjoying it! "I challenge you to even come up with one such instance," Ganapatiji continued to taunt his colleague in the meanwhile.

"Ganapatiji, as I said, I am not sure at all whether what I am going to say next is relevant in our case at all, but please hear me out before you bury me alive," Sanjay said. And then, looking at everyone seated in the room, he continued. "Some of you may know my house is adjacent to our city's fire station. I have rarely seen the fire engine vehicles being used for doing the job it is expected to do, although I see a lot of the people there cleaning it, checking its engine, and otherwise spending a lot of time and money ensuring that it will work smoothly and do its job when it is called upon to do so. Now, isn't that a classic example of a costly machine just lying idle most of the time but is still a valuable asset? On the other hand, aren't all of us really happy that it is not constantly put to use? There are 6 fire engines there, and each one has a designated driver. Of these, I know 2 drivers personally. You will be surprised to know the cost of these trucks and the cost of maintaining them!"

"And long may they remain idle," said Chandra, the Sales Head, folding his hands in prayer. "I am perfectly fine to see these drivers lounging around the fire station or doing other jobs there. Imagine the state of our city if these men are the most productive people around!" he shuddered in fear.

"Hmm, ok. Agreed. It is better for all of us if these trucks are not running up and down our roads," Ganapatiji acknowledged in a diplomatic tone.

"Fantastic point," TOC Guru burst into the conversation. "Sanjayji, you are on fire! Pardon the poor pun, but tell me, why do you think this won't be applicable in your organization's case? I know that all of you are 'fire-fighting' the whole day, but that alone is not the point of similarity," he said to the amusement of his audience.

"Can we apply this insight, this learning, into our company also? What I mean to say is — is it imperative that all of our resources need to be put into use regularly? Can't we let our resources rest for a while without making them feel guilty? Or making ourselves feel guilty? Do we have to be like the slave drivers of yore? Surely, some of these resources at least can remain idle for some time now and then?"

"Good question, TOC Guru. You have given us food for thought," Sanjay remarked.

"Food for thought reminds me," said Ganapatiji, looking at his watch. "My digestive system has been remaining idle for a while now. I need to put that into use. How about we break now and get something to eat? It is 9 pm and way past my dinner time."

TOC Guru let out a loud laugh and got up from his seat. The others followed him.

Naresh said, "Absolutely. Let's refuel ourselves and come back tomorrow, shall we? I think we are making fantastic progress here, and thank you, TOC Guru and Abhinav for leading these discussions. Gentlemen, how about 09:30 am tomorrow?" The group concurred and trooped out of the conference room, with Ganapatiji putting his arm around Sanjay and discussing the cost of fire engines!

Chapter 11

The Treasure Hunt

The group was back at the appointed time at 9:30 am. Naresh was delighted to see the enthusiasm of his team members. That Saturday was their Founder's Day, and a holiday, but all of them were more than happy to assemble and analyze their problems and see how they could resolve it with the help of TOC Guru and Abhinav.

As usual, it was Ganapatiji who kick-started the discussion by coming straight to the point. "TOC Guru, today we should really dig deep and come to a conclusion whether a resource, in fact, many precious resources, standing idle is a major waste or not. I really cannot believe that this is even up for debate, but I am willing to consider this possibility after our fire engine discussion yesterday."

"Thank you, Ganapatiji, for allowing all of us to proceed without having to refer to our minutes of the meeting," acknowledged TOC Guru with a loud chuckle. "That is precisely what we will look at today. But, to do that, we will have to play a game, a simulation game."

"What all will you make us do, TOC Guru!" complained Ganapatiji but in good humor.

TOC Guru helped himself to a cup of coffee and walked over to the whiteboard placed at one end of the conference room. He started scribbling some notes there.

"Gentlemen, here are the facts that we should consider:

- There are 5 resources (A, B, C, D, and E).

- A is the RM feeding and E the FG conversion.

- B, C, and D are the resources required to process the WIP.

- We roll dice to simulate the capacities.

- A, B, D, and E have 2 dice. And, since a dice has a maximum number of 6, they can potentially have a value of 12 each time they roll the dice. And, this is the maximum capacity that these resources can have.

- C, on the other hand, has only one die."

TOC Guru paused and looked around at his audience. "Are you all with me up till now?" he asked. Although his audience was curious as to where TOC Guru was taking them all toward, they nodded their heads in agreement.

TOC Guru continued. "Good. Let me explain with a few possible scenarios to make this clearer. For example, if we roll the 2 dice together, and the number 5 appeared on both the dice, what is the final figure?"

"10, I can answer this without an Excel or a calculator," came the response promptly from Sanjay Malhotra, the Finance Head.

The others laughed at this self-deprecatory humor from the Finance Head.

"Brilliant," said TOC Guru with a twinkle in his eye. "That was not a difficult question. From a production perspective, however, what does this number mean?" he asked, looking around at the group seated in front of him.

"TOC Guru, that represents the available capacity for the day," Ganapatiji ventured to respond.

"Then, what is this 12 that we are getting by rolling 2 dice?" Chandra, the Sales and Marketing Head, had a query. "That is the rated capacity for that resource, while the actual figure we get by rolling is the capacity for the day," TOC Guru chipped in.

"Aha, then this is similar to our company, where the available capacity may change based on power shutdown/maintenance shutdown, absenteeism, etc.," Ganapatiji correlated with his experience. TOC Guru nodded in agreement.

He continued. "Now, there are WIPs to be tackled. Let us consider a WIP of 6 in front of all the resources. Based on the number each resource got while rolling the dice, it has to move the WIP to the next resource. Let us denote this as the production process."

He paused, looked around the room, and said, "Listen to me carefully now. When one resource got 5 each on each of its dice, meaning 10 in total, as the available capacity, and with a WIP of

6, how much can they process? Meaning, how much can they send to the next resource?"

"Obviously 6," Naresh chimed in.

"Exactly, because 10 - 6 = 4. And, 4 is the loss of output," added Ganapatiji quickly.

"Well done," cried TOC Guru, encouraging the group in front of him.

"Let us consider another scenario. What will happen if the rolled number is 8, and you have a WIP of 8?" TOC Guru asked the team.

"We move all 8 to the next resource," Mathew, the Procurement Head, chimed in.

"Exactly. Because, with a capacity of 8, moving less than the available capacity leads to poor capacity utilization of the respective resource," Sanjay, the Finance Head, added.

"True. This is because resource efficiency is the operating paradigm," Ganapatiji agreed by nodding his head.

TOC Guru continued. "Here are the rules of the game," and he requested Abhinav to go and write down his points on the whiteboard.

A   B   C   D   E
1. Rated capacity = 12 (if 2 dice) | 6 (if 1 dice)
2. Available capacity = based on the number you get after rolling the dice
3. Output = based on WiP moved to the next resource
4. Capacity utilization (resource efficiency) is the operating paradigm.

1. Rated capacity = 12 (if 2 dice) | 6 (if 1 dice)

2. Available capacity = based on the number you get after rolling the dice

3. Output = based on WIP moved to the next resource

4. Capacity utilization (resource efficiency) is the operating paradigm.

Abhinav quickly summarized the learning so far on the whiteboard.

"Gentlemen, it is now time to play the dice game," TOC Guru said. From his laptop bag, he took out some dice and a bag of pebbles, the sort that is used in fish tanks. He kept them on the table.

Now, Sanjay (Finance) – Chandra (Sales and Marketing) – Ganapatiji (Production) – Mathew (Procurement) – and Naresh (PPC) sat similar to A, B, C, D, and E drawn on the board…

Abhinav handed them dice. Ganapatiji received 1, while all the others received 2 each. TOC Guru then placed 6 pebbles in front of all the resources, except the first resource – Finance, represented by Sanjay. There, he kept all the balance pebbles.

"Let us play a trial round first and once all of you are comfortable, we will begin the game in earnest, all right?" suggested TOC Guru.

"This reminds me of my street cricket days while in school," chuckled Mathew, the Procurement Head.

TOC Guru let out a loud laugh. "All right, gentlemen. We start from right to left. That is, Naresh gets to roll his dice first. He will move the WIP to the next resource. He will be followed by the upstream resources."

Within a few rounds, all of them became comfortable rolling the dice and moving the WIP to the downstream resource based on the number that appeared when they rolled their dice.

"Good, good. Now, let us play for real, gentlemen. This is where the rubber meets the road. All set?" asked TOC Guru.

"Absolutely," said Ganapatiji. "What TOC Guru? You are making us feel as if we are part of 'Ocean's Eleven' or something!" This was met with laughter from the whole group.

"Why not, Clooney Ganapatiji? We will play a T20 match out of this. Meaning, 20 rounds where each round will represent one day. So, a total of 20 days. We will see where we end up at the end of that period. Abhinav here will be our Master Scorer."

Turning to Abhinav, he added, "Please note down the number of rounds, the WIP moved at every work center per round, and the final output post the last resource, Naresh." Abhinav nodded his head in agreement and quickly opened an Excel file on his laptop.

"So long as I am not placing any bets, and as long as there is no Shakuni Maama among us, I am fine," Chandra's remark was met with loud laughs, and the group set out to play the dice game with great enthusiasm. They rolled back all the WIP to the first resource (Finance Head), leaving 6 as process WIP in front of the other resources.

As they progressed through the rounds, TOC Guru noticed a few other employees trooping into the conference room. "Word has gotten out that the leaders are playing dice games instead of working," he chuckled and remarked to Abhinav. "Absolutely, and I heard one of the guys quip to his friend that with some luck, they would get to see a few blows being exchanged between Ganapatiji and Mathew today!" Abhinav responded with a wry smile. And, when the WIP started piling up in front of Ganapatiji, the Production Head, there was a lot of excitement among the audience.

The group completed 20 rounds in approximately 25 minutes. Abhinav was ready with his observations.

He projected the Excel data as shown below.

Scenario 1:	**Total Output**	72
	WIP	86

"Gentlemen, here is my question to you. With a maximum possible capacity or resource of 12, and with 20 rounds, the output should have been around 240; any idea why it was just 72?" TOC Guru triggered the discussion further.

"But naturally, and isn't it obvious why that is the case, TOC Guru?" piped Mathew. "The capacity at resource C was only 6, and the output of this production set-up was determined by the lowest capacity resource, Ganapatiji."

Ganapatiji squirmed in his seat and added rather defensively, "And, I observed that many times, I had more WIP, but a lesser number than 6 on the dice. Meaning that my average output was around 3 or 4."

"Exactly, as all of you no doubt know, statistical average is (n + 1) / 2 = (6 + 1) / 2 = 3.5, where n is the maximum that you can get by rolling a dice. And," and here, TOC Guru gave a sympathetic look toward Ganapatiji, "we gave only one dice to Ganapatiji here, that is, resource C." After adding this statistical flavor to the discussion, TOC Guru kept quiet, waiting for one of the Managers to take the discussion forward.

"Ah, ok, now I understand why the output was around 70. An average of 3.5 per round, and we played 20 rounds. So, when we multiply these 2, we get 70," (3.5 avg. per round X 20 rounds = 70), chipped in Mathew, the Procurement Head.

"Very good, Mr. Mathew. Now that you have understood how we got the output, let us try and see how we can calculate the production lead time," TOC Guru continued.

"20 rounds?" Chandra, the Sales Head asked tentatively.

"I am afraid not. That was the number of rounds that we played. Production lead time means when the order will come out of the last resource when you start an order," Ganapatiji gleefully tried to correct his colleague.

Apart from Ganapatiji, however, no one else was really convinced by this point. There were some murmurs among the audience, but no one was able to come out with a clear answer, until Naresh spoke up. "If my memory serves me right, from my MBA days, I recall that the lead time has something to do with WIP," he paused, but gathering confidence seeing TOC Guru nodding his head vigorously, he added. "Is this called 'Little's Law' by any chance?"

"Superb, Naresh. Clearly you were an excellent student then as well as now!" TOC Guru complimented Naresh. "When you divide the WIP by the average output, you will get the lead time. Meaning, if WIP = 86 and the average output = 3.5, the production lead time = 86 / 3.5 = 24.5 days," Abhinav calculated using his Excel and wrote this down on the whiteboard.

	Total Output	72
Scenario 1	**WIP**	86
	Production Lead Time	25 days

"Excellent, but surely there are more conclusions to be drawn from our historic dice game, gentlemen?" TOC Guru was relentless. There was silence while the managers tried to wrap their heads around this question. After a while, Sanjay, the Finance Head observed, "Upstream resources - like me and Chandra here - were efficient; but downstream resources after Ganapatiji were starving most of the time."

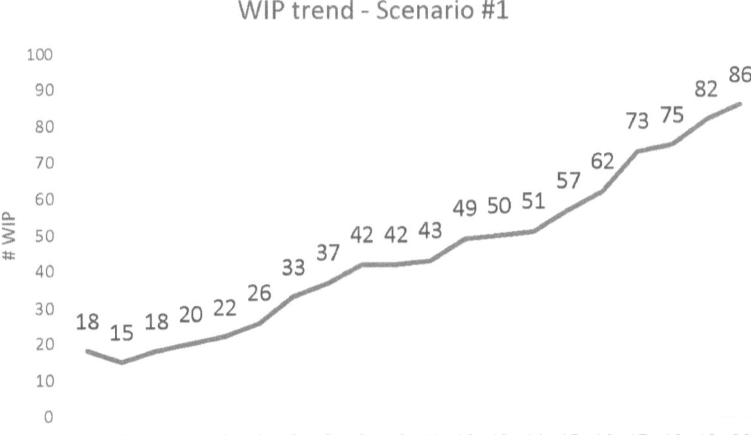

"Exactly, if this would have been the case in real life, I would have kissed goodbye to any realistic hopes I might have had of ever getting a promotion, as my KRA is based on how efficient I am in meeting my production targets," Mathew said loudly, thumping the table in front of him.

"Significant WIP was stuck with resource C," Naresh mused, voicing the thoughts in everyone's minds.

"What am I to do, yaar? I am like the hapless spinner introduced during the powerplay in a T20 against 2 batsmen hell-bent on destroying the cricket ball. I get one dice, while all of you get 2, and the problem is with the way I manage my work!" Ganapatiji looked crestfallen.

No one bothered to respond to this, much to Ganapatiji's chagrin.

"Also, because this high WIP is stuck with resource C, most of the production lead time should belong to this waiting time," Chandra, the Sales Head added logically.

"Yes, indeed," TOC Guru jumped back into the discussion. "In fact, the production lead time has 2 components:

1. Waiting Time, and

2. Process Time

Abhinav wrote these terms on the whiteboard. TOC Guru continued, "Waiting time meaning how much time the order is waiting to get into the resource for processing, while process time means how much time it takes for the order to be processed by the resource."

"In that case, taking a clue from what we observed from this dice game, waiting time should be the significant portion of production lead times," Chandra said, continuing with his logical reasoning.

"Good point," TOC Guru encouraged him. "Also, this is applicable almost in all production environments, as long as we manage them in real time as we did in this dice game!"

"Managing production as we managed this dice game? I don't understand, can you explain more?" Ganapatiji looked puzzled.

"Absolutely. What was the management paradigm that all of us intuitively deployed here?" TOC Guru asked.

"Utilizing the resources as much as possible?" Ganapatiji asked doubtfully.

"Yes, I think so. As long as we had WIP, we produced to the full available capacity for that round at every resource," Naresh added.

"Hmm, yes. But what about the output? Even though we produced to the full available capacities of individual resources, the overall output was determined by resource C, and the flow of WIP got really slow at resource C," Sanjay added.

"There, again. Giving me just one dice, and then putting all the blame on me!" Ganapatiji muttered to himself.

TOC Guru chuckled on hearing this but added, "Absolutely. And, this is the most predominant production management paradigm in almost every organization, and hence, high WIP contributes to high waiting time compared with the actual process time. In my experience, waiting constitutes about 80% to 90% of the total production lead time."

That was a shocking insight for the team.

"Then, TOC Guru, how should we manage production then?" Mathew, the Procurement Head asked the question that seemed to be in everyone's minds.

"Well, gentlemen, that needs some deep thinking, and I find that I don't do that very well when all I can think of is food!" TOC Guru said, laughing loudly.

"Of course, of course," Naresh seemed apologetic. The game and the discussions were so engrossing for all of them that no one had noticed how long they had been at it. "My bad, TOC Guru. Why don't we break for lunch now and then continue to ponder over these questions!"

"Excellent suggestion, Naresh," TOC Guru said, getting up on his feet. "How about continuing the discussion in 45 minutes? That, I think, will give me enough time to do a quality inspection of all the items in your superb canteen!"

Abhinav and Naresh exchanged smiles on hearing this, and everyone started moving toward the canteen.

Chapter 12

Play (Game) to Learn

After having a light lunch, the managers took some time to interact with their teams, clear their inboxes, etc. Finally, everyone was back in the conference rooms by 3 pm, 15 minutes later than the agreed upon time. Ganapatiji seemed intent to make up for lost time, and even before all of them were properly settled and ready to resume the discussion, he jumped straight into the thick of things.

"TOC Guru, during our pre-lunch discussion, we understood that it was resource C, meaning Capacity Constraint Resource (CCR), that determined the output of the unit."

Mathew, the Procurement Head, interrupted his colleague. "This means that if we use resource CCR fully, the output can be protected, isn't it?"

"And, that, in turn, means that utilizing other resources, meaning non-CCR, is akin to drinking water from a mirage," Sanjay, the Finance Head joined the discussion.

TOC Guru beamed at everyone around. "My, my! Lunch does seem to have done its job, isn't it?" Abhinav and Naresh grinned at him.

"If I may," added Naresh. "Now that we seemed to have gained a deeper understanding of the fundamental flaw in our current operating paradigm, how should we manage the dice game then?"

"Wait a second, TOC Guru. It looks like common sense now," Sanjay was not prepared to let TOC Guru steal the show if he could help it. "It appears to me that CCR should work to its full efficiency, while other resources, non-CCRs, should work as per CCR."

"That is easier said than done, Sanjay, Sir," cut in Mathew. "How do we make it happen? Tell us that!"

"Again, it is common sense, isn't it?" This time it was Ganapatiji. "Simply starve them. I mean, don't give more work to non-CCRs."

"Let me get this straight," interrupted Naresh. "You are advocating giving them less work?" Naresh asked with a hint of sarcasm in his voice.

All this while TOC Guru was happy to let the group carry on with their discussion, quietly sipping a cup of freshly made coffee.

Ganapatiji seemed a little flustered hearing Naresh's question. He shifted uneasily in his chair and said, "Well, I did not mean that. I meant, don't give them more work or less work either."

Everyone looked astonished. What was Ganapatiji saying? Their sense of optimism at having cracked this vexing problem seemed to be receding. "Now, we are all confused. I have no idea where you are going with this, Ganapatiji. First, you seemed to suggest that non-CCR should not be given more work even if they can handle it. Now you are saying don't give them less work either. Are you saying that we continue the way we are doing right now? And, pray, how will that solve our problems?" Sanjay took out his frustration at his senior colleague, who seemed to have lost the plot for the first time during this entire discussion.

TOC Guru was studiously avoiding looking at anyone's eyes. His coffee seemed to have gotten his complete attention. Abhinav knew that this was all part of his esteemed colleague's sense of drama. After a few seconds of silence, TOC Guru pretended to come out of a reverie and exclaimed. "Oh! You folks need my help? What happened? I thought you had almost solved the puzzle! Very well then. Let me see where and how I can help you," he said, putting his cup down on the table.

"If I understood you correctly, Ganapatiji, all you were trying to suggest was that give work to non-CCR resources as per the output of resource C. If resource C gives you more output, other resources more that day, and vice versa?" TOC Guru looked at Ganapatiji quizzically, while the others nodded their heads in agreement, as if to say that that made total sense.

"Well, er, yes," spluttered Ganapatiji. "That is exactly what I said. I don't know why any of them could not understand it. You say the same thing – well, maybe, you put it in fancier words – and they all swallow it. How ridiculous!"

TOC Guru laughed out loud. "Absolutely, absolutely true. Beats me too, Ganapatiji!"

The mood around the room suddenly seemed to have lifted by a notch or 2. They were back in business.

"What are the tactics to do this then?" wondered Naresh aloud, remembering some of the jargons he had heard during his MBA days.

"The tactics, Nareshji, are quite clear. But, let me try and use some fancy verbiage this time. That might make it palatable to the august audience in this room," said Ganapatiji sarcastically. "While releasing the RM at resource A, the quantity of release should be the same as resource C's output." He looked to see if TOC Guru was impressed with this.

"Now you hit the nail on its head with precision," TOC Guru jumped up from his chair in excitement. Ganapatiji looked very pleased with himself, while the rest of the team digested this new insight.

"So, are you going to propose another round of the dice game, TOC Guru, but this time we play with the understanding of this new paradigm?" Chandra, who was quiet for a while, asked.

"Absolutely," said TOC Guru, nodding his head at Abhinav. Abhinav understood what TOC Guru was asking him to do. He immediately opened his laptop and got ready to note down the details of runs similar to round 1. The others started moving closer to the table to have another go at the dice game.

"We start from right to left, the same way as the previous round," TOC Guru instructed. "So, our friend here, Naresh, will start rolling the dice and move the WIP to the next resource, followed by upstream resources, ok?"

"We are aware of the rules of the game by now, TOC Guru. I get to roll one dice while the others have fun with 2!" Ganapatiji was back to his original self.

"Of course, of course. My bad. No doubt you have understood that for this round you get the chance to gloat over someone else, right?" TOC Guru winked at Abhinav while he was handing over the dice to the participants. Ganapatiji looked a bit puzzled but tried not to show it. Abhinav understood what his senior wanted of him. He gave one die to Ganapatiji, and 2 each to all the other resources. But when the Finance Head, Sanjay, extended his hand to collect his die, Abhinav gave him a big smile and said, "No die for you this time around, Sir!"

"Wah," Sanjay exclaimed loudly. "You want me to participate in a dice game but without a die?" he seemed disappointed.

Ganapatiji seemed to have understood the rules of this round. He quickly piped up. "Arrey, Sir. We discussed this, na? RM release is as only per resource CCR's output. Meaning, your release quantity is as per my output," he said, laughing delightedly, realizing that he could lord over someone else in his team finally!

"Oh, ok. So, this is not an exact replica of round 1?" Sanjay seemed a bit puzzled.

"Exactly, and before anyone has a related query – no, there are no more changes. All the other rules remain the same. Meaning, we will play 20 rounds, where one round will represent one day, and so a total of 20 days," TOC Guru elucidated for the benefit of all in the room. "And, Abhinav, here will again help us by acting as our Master Scorer."

Saying this, TOC Guru turned toward his younger colleague and said, "Abhinav, please note down the number of rounds, WIP moved at every work center per round, and the final output post the last resource, exactly as before, please. And, Naresh, please kick off this round too, as before!"

Abhinav gave a thumbs-up to TOC Guru to indicate that he was ready. The others also gave a thumbs-up, and the group started playing the game with some excitement, curious to know what the results would be this time around!

This time they completed the game quickly – only 20 minutes to complete all 20 rounds. Abhinav took a couple of minutes to finalize the results and then displayed them to his audience.

Scenario 2:	Total Output	73
	WIP	23

"Wow! almost the same output as before, but look at the WIP!" Ganapatiji sounded elated. "From a whopping 86 to a measly 23! Fantastic!"

"Anything else, gentlemen?" TOC Guru looked around the table. "And, no, it doesn't have to be tangible, objective data all the time either!" he encouraged them.

"Hmm, did anyone else feel this? I somehow felt calmer this time around. The environment seemed more peaceful, if I can use that word for a game!" Mathew added a bit tentatively.

"I don't know about 'peaceful,' Mathew, but the flow was smooth. And, did we not complete this round quickly?" Sanjay asked, looking at Abhinav, who nodded his head in agreement.

"This means that the lead time should also have come down drastically," Naresh added, referring to Little's Law.

"Absolutely, my friend," said Abhinav. "With the WIP at 23 and the average output remaining the same as before, viz., 3.5, the production lead time = 23 / 3.5 = 7 days." He then showed the updated table to everyone in the room.

	Total Output	73
Scenario 2	**WIP**	23
	Production Lead Time	7

"Wow! more than 50% reduction in lead time, while giving the same output, almost," Ganapatiji could not contain his excitement as he leaped out of his chair.

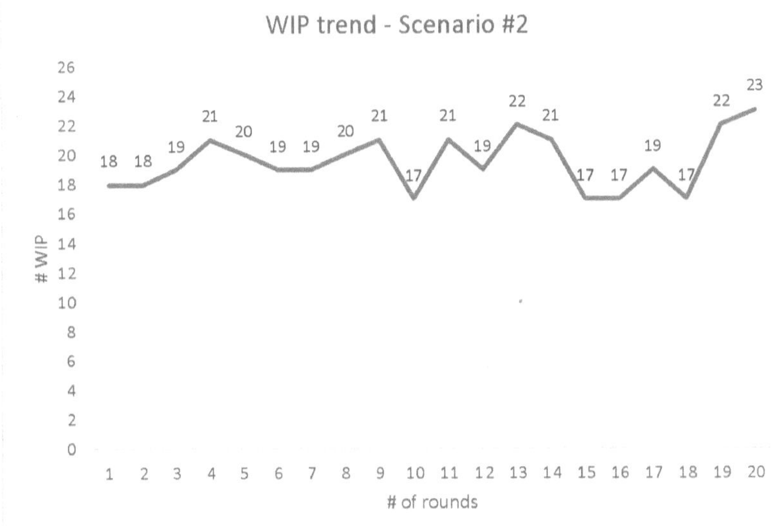

"Ganapatiji, please don't give me a heart attack," Sanjay said, laughing. "But coming to this round, mind you, this is with the average output of 3.5 at resource C, the CCR. And, if we need more output overall, I know which projects to approve – projects that increase the output of CCR," he winked at his colleagues.

Everyone laughed at hearing this. Naresh added, "Although you said this as a sort of joke, that is an excellent point, Sanjay."

Mathew interrupted Naresh at this point. "What this really means is that resource C should be the one to be utilized efficiently, and not all the resources, isn't it?"

"Precisely," this time it was Sanjay who jumped out of his seat. "Taking this forward, the conclusion we can draw is that the core conflict cloud we started the morning discussion with - where we were challenging that resource standing idle is a major waste - is applicable only to CCR, isn't it?" He was feeling rather proud of the fact that he had thought of the example of the fire engines lying idle.

"You are absolutely right, Sanjayji," TOC Guru agreed.

"Wait a minute," Ganapatiji interrupted. "If resource C has to be utilized efficiently, meaning, efficiency is the prime measure for CCR, what about the non-CCRs then, eh? How do we measure non CCRs then?"

"The wily fox does not want to make it a walk in the park for the other heads," TOC Guru thought to himself with a chuckle. But he did not say anything, looking to see if any of the other department heads came up with the right response to this query.

"Relax, Ganapatiji. We are not implying that non-CCRs should not be measured at all. All that we are saying is that non CCRs should not work on WIP that is not required by CCR. Otherwise, it only creates excess WIP and increases the waiting time significantly. Therefore, non-CCRs should effectively work only on WIP that is required by CCR," Mathew added but without really answering Ganapatiji's question.

"So, not efficiency, but effectiveness should be the prime measure for non – CCRs," Sanjay said, but he did not sound quite confident and so turned to look at TOC Guru.

"Absolutely, Sanjayji. Why are you sounding tentative?" TOC Guru exclaimed, giving the table a loud thump. He continued, "Release work as per CCR output. The prime measure for CCR = efficiency, and the prime measure for non CCRs = effectiveness. It is clear as day!"

Naresh caught the excitement and quickly went to the board, and summarized the new operating paradigm and new measures.

"And, obviously this leads to improved flow and reduced lead time. Meaning, we will be able to complete orders on time and even ahead of schedule if we are able to increase the output of CCR, isn't it?" Chandra, the Sales Head could see his fondest wishes finally looking not completely like a pipe dream.

"There you go, Mr. Chandra. You will get what you most fervently wished for!" TOC Guru patted him on his back.

There was a moment or 2 of silence as the group digested all these insights.

The reverie was broken by Ganapatiji, loudly clearing his throat. "All that is wonderful, but how do we deploy these new learnings to our environment?"

TOC Guru gave a loud chuckle. "Well, that is an excellent question, as usual, from our friend, Ganapatiji; but now it is half-past 6 p.m. And I stop working exactly at 6 p.m. I need to spend some time with my books and my music to recharge my batteries. I know it is Sunday tomorrow, but I can make myself available to try and find a solution to Ganapatiji's query and a few others; but what about you gentlemen?" he asked, looking around the room. Since Sunday was the only weekly holiday they got to get away from work and spend some time with their family, TOC Guru was not sure what the response would be.

"Oh yes. No problem. We seem to be on the verge of a breakout. I say we push forward and crack this problem wide open," said Chandra. All the others nodded their heads in agreement.

"Fantastic," said Naresh, looking delighted. "I feel that tomorrow will be a game-changing day for all of us. If you are willing to stretch yourself on a Sunday, we will, of course, be delighted to work and close this out. So, shall we meet at 10 a.m.?" he asked, looking at TOC Guru, Abhinav, and also his entire team.

"Absolutely," said Ganapatiji on behalf of his team. TOC Guru and Abhinav smiled, seeing the energy levels of the team, and packed their laptop, cables, etc. The team walked out of the room, with TOC Guru explaining how he managed to wake up daily by 3:30 a.m. by hitting the bed by 8:45 p.m. and also eating his dinner before 7:30 p.m., with Sanjay nodding his head in appreciation.

Chapter 13

Dinner Date

On his way out, Naresh suddenly felt quite optimistic. He decided to call Priya. He was feeling quite guilty about not returning her call earlier that day. "What am I to do? With my professional front in such shambles, I was in no frame of mind to talk to anyone," he tried to justify his behavior, but knew deep down that this was not a good excuse. However, his feeling that a solution to his professional problems was round the corner was so strong that he continued to be in a good mood.

"Hey, Priya," he said cheerfully when Priya picked up the phone. Priya said "Hi," but there was no real warmth in her greeting. Naresh decided to ignore that and went ahead. "What are you doing this evening? Shall we go out to that Italian restaurant you have been raving about? I feel like eating a Spaghetti Aglio e Olio. In fact, I have been dreaming of this dish for so long that I can actually smell the garlic in olive oil just now!"

"What is the matter with you? Are you alright? Have you got a fever or something?" asked Priya a bit sarcastically. "I thought you were only interested in dal rice. Think the last time you ate anything non-Indian was during our college farewell. Better go and consult a doctor or something."

"I know, I know, Priya. I have been preoccupied, I admit. It is not as if I am unaware of this. And I concede quite easily that you have been patience personified. I am truly sorry. But listen, I truly believe that I can see a few slivers of light at the end of the tunnel. This TOC Guru is a godsend, I think. Plus, all of my colleagues are also collaborating magnificently, and we are on the verge of making a breakthrough," Naresh continued, his voice ringing with excitement.

Priya couldn't help but notice a sense of relief in Naresh's voice. But things were not going smoothly for her at her house. She, however, softened her tone a bit and said, "Ok, sure. Let's go to this restaurant. I was meaning to tell you something anyway." Naresh became a bit apprehensive on hearing this but did not pursue the matter. Better to have this conversation face-to-face, he thought.

On reaching home, Naresh quickly took a bath and chose a shirt that Priya had gifted him for his previous birthday. On the way, he decided to stop and buy a book that Priya was praising, hoping that she had not bought it herself. Inside that, he wrote, "Priya, nothing but love and gratitude. Thank you for being there!" The shopkeeper glanced at it while gift-wrapping the book and smiled knowingly at Naresh. "Sir, if she is going to forgive you with just this one book, you are truly a lucky man. Hope you keep buying books from here, although I would be happier to see the 2 of you come in to our shop together and buy 2 books at a time!" he let out a big laugh at his own joke. Naresh merely smiled and made the payment and quickly got back into his car. He didn't want to be late for his date.

The traffic was not as bad as he had anticipated, and Naresh reached the restaurant a few minutes before the appointed time. He chose a table that overlooked the beautifully manicured lawns. "The full moon is a bonus," he chuckled. Calling the waiter over, he quickly ordered Priya's favorite starter, the bruschetta with tomatoes and basil.

A few minutes later, Priya walked in. "God, she is so stunning," Naresh couldn't help noticing how simple and elegant she looked. He also noticed a few heads turning her way. "Yup, I am a lucky guy indeed. Beauty, brains, and a loving heart. I must not lose her. God, what an idiot I have been?" he thought to himself while signaling to her. He noticed the slightly startled look on Priya's face.

She came and settled herself down. "You are early, for a change?" she said a bit sarcastically. "And, I see you still have that shirt that I gave you?"

Naresh merely smiled and handed over the gift-wrapped book. "What is this? Your TOC Guru's autobiography?" she continued with the teasing. "Open it and see. Er, just read the first page. The rest you can read later, ok?" Naresh tried to lighten the mood.

"Oh, this one? I told you about this 6 months back. You didn't think I would have gotten a copy myself? Anyway, thanks," she said, putting it in her bag without opening the book. Naresh felt a wave of disappointment and cursed himself. The waiter appeared with the bruschetta, and Priya's eyes lit up. "Ha, at least this one didn't take 6 months? Thanks. I was feeling quite hungry." She started eating the starter with great relish, and soon a look of contentment spread across her face.

Naresh waited for her to speak. After a few minutes of silence, Priya said quietly, "Naresh, I know that things are not going well for you at your work front. I am truly sorry to know this, and I have been patient." Naresh opened his mouth to say something, but she continued quickly, "No, hear me out. I don't know what you expect from me. You don't let me into your problems either. It is not as if I am an illiterate person. I too have the same degree as you, you know? Anyway, be that as it may, what I have to tell you is this. My folks are getting impatient. They want to know what your intentions are. I have kept them at bay for more than a year now, but now, even I am beginning to wonder if you truly intend to take our relationship forward."

Naresh was taken aback by the matter of fact tone with which Priya said this. He realized that mere platitudes wouldn't work, not that he was dragging his feet deliberately. He, however, recognized that the issue was not just the one pertaining to his job. Priya had, for the first time, openly talked about an aspect of his personality that he himself was worried about. Years of being the sole breadwinner for his family, of being there for the others in his family both financially and emotionally, had meant that he had built an armor around himself. Appearing to be vulnerable had not been an option for him. He did not want to become someone who hesitated to ask for help; but circumstances were such.

He took a sip of water and said, "Priya, I do recognize the truth in what you are saying. No other girl would have waited for this long, I am certain of that. I, however, hope that you recognize that I need to feel settled in this job before I become part of your family, just as you will become a part of mine."

Priya sighed. "We have gone through this a number of times, Naresh. Don't blame me if I happen to come from a 'highly successful' family. I don't subscribe to their worldview regarding success, etc. But I also realize that it is important for you to feel comfortable in your own skin. But tell me, how do we proceed from here? We can't keep going in circles, that is for sure."

"Yes," cried Naresh passionately. "I understand that you are not like your family, and believe me, there is pressure from my family too. But, okay, let us not go over the grounds that we have already covered. I wanted to tell you about the progress we are making with TOC Guru coming in and analyzing our situation. The man is a godsend, truly."

"They were interrupted by the waiter who came to clear their plates and checked if they were ready with their orders for the main course. Priya looked at the menu, while Naresh placed his order of Spaghetti Aglio e Olio. After a few seconds, she ordered a Caprese Salad with Pesto Sauce. The waiter noted down their orders and took his leave.

"Ok, so tell me. What is this TOC Guru doing? And why do you think this time it is going to be different for you and your organization? This is not the first external consultant your company has hired."

"Yes, you are right about the second part, but to be honest, we didn't hire this TOC Guru. He is doing all this for free! How is he different? Well, he is nothing like the previous consultants. He listens more, doesn't offer a ready-made solution, lets us bumble our way around, and steps in only when he feels we are going completely off track. And, he gets us, each one of us. And, Abhinav swears by him. So, yeah, I think this time we are really going to emerge out of the tunnel."

Naresh then began to outline what had happened till then and what the next steps would be. Meanwhile, the waiter arrived with their food. The aroma of garlic, olive oil, fresh basil, tomatoes tickled their senses, and the young couple eagerly started tucking into their food. Priya asked Naresh a couple of questions, and very soon, their tension evaporated a bit. Wiping her mouth with a napkin, Priya said, "Great news, Naresh. I now believe that your optimism is not misplaced." She paused for a few seconds and then added, "But then what is the next step for us?"

Naresh sighed but added quickly, "Priya, I beseech you not to think of what I am going to say next as yet another attempt on my part to drag my feet. Believe me, it hurts me as much as it hurts you. But all I am asking is for 2 more months. And then I am at your disposal. Whatever you decide, wherever you want to get married, whoever you want to call, blah, blah, blah!"

Priya laughed. "Phew, glad you stopped after those 3 and didn't add with whoever you want to get married!" Naresh laughed at hearing this. "No, never. That spot is reserved for me, and only me!"

Exactly at that moment, the waiter arrived with the dessert menu. Both of them decided to share a portion of Tiramisu. "Excellent choice, Madam," the waiter smiled at Priya. "We believe that ours is the finest in this city."

"Excellent," said Naresh with a smile. And after the waiter left, he said, "Did you know that Tiramisu means…"

"Ah, yes, 'cheer me up' or something like that, isn't it?" Priya interrupted him. Naresh nodded his head in agreement.

"In that case, we should have ordered 2 plates of TOC Guru," said Priya with a grin. Naresh laughed heartily hearing this. He felt as if a weight had been removed from his chest."

Chapter 14

Learn to Play (Real)

The day was a bit cooler than the previous few days, with a gentle breeze energizing everyone. Naresh had had a good chat with Priya and felt really upbeat. "Might rain a bit," he thought to himself as he sipped his coffee while looking out of the window. "I really hope we get to the bottom of all our problems." He was feeling quite proud of his team as well, the way they collaborated with each other to go to the bottom of their challenges. "Thank goodness I decided to go to that college reunion and bumped into Abhinav. I must remember to thank Priya too," he made a mental note as it was Priya who kept nudging him to join her. He had not been in any frame of mind to participate in that get together initially.

The whole team was ready to continue their discussion by 9.45 am although it was a Sunday. TOC Guru and Abhinav joined them soon afterward. Within a few minutes, they were both ready. Naresh made sure that TOC Guru's coffee was piping hot, the way he liked it. He then set the ball rolling by reminding the agenda for that day.

"Gentlemen, our objective today is to discuss how we can convert yesterday's FLOW learnings from round 2 of the dice game to our production environment."

"Exactly," Ganapatiji took the discussion forward. "And, I guess the first question for us to consider is – what is resource C for us? Meaning, what is the CCR for us?"

"Technically yes, but," TOC Guru barely got these 3 words out before he was interrupted by the others trying to answer Ganapatiji's question. "Dyeing," "What rubbish, it is definitely spinning," "No, it is warping, I feel," etc. could be heard.

Naresh laughed and jumped in. "Woah, hold on guys. Very interesting to see that almost all the key work centers are getting posited as the CCR; but surely, that cannot be right?" he said looking at TOC Guru.

"Precisely the problem, and thank you Naresh for pointing that out," TOC Guru said chuckling. "The best person to identify the CCR is...," and here he paused, "the CCR itself," he finished with a wink, much to the confusion of the others in the room.

Abhinav was watching his senior's performance very keenly. "God, he sure knows how to let the audience eat out of his hands. Look at their confused expressions, poor guys!" he thought to himself feeling sorry for their plight. "Don't worry guys. No one even understands the TOC Guru's jokes, forget appreciating it at the first instant."

"The CCR will identify itself? What exactly does that even mean? Sorry, this is a bouncer even for a six-footer!" Ganapatiji said scratching his head.

"How did we know what the CCR was in our dice game?" TOC Guru probed further.

"By giving that resource only one dice?" Sanjay, the Finance Head asked doubtfully.

"And also, that was the resource where more WIP was getting accumulated in round 1 of our dice game. And that obstructed the flow of fish tank pebbles, I mean, orders," Naresh remarked.

"Great going guys," TOC Guru encouraged the cohort. "Precisely the point that I was hoping to get from all of you. So, if there is a CCR on the shop floor, what should have been the indicator?" He put the next question forward.

Abhinav was marveling at the way his senior was leading the discussion forward.

"Oh, I got it," Ganapatiji was quick to reply. "What you are suggesting is that there will be high WIP in front of the CCR." But then he paused as he considered the scenario. "Hmm, let us forget the dice game for a second. In our organization, there are high WIPs in front of almost every work center, and the flow is obstructed everywhere. So, are all our resources CCRs?"

"That is an interesting question, Ganapatiji," TOC Guru remarked. "In a river, for example, there could be many obstructions. Rocks of varying sizes, stones, vegetation, etc., but that does not mean that water stops flowing altogether, right? It would flow slowly above and around these obstructions. And, if you want to improve the flow of the river further, what will you do?"

"Oh, that is very simple," Mathew, the Procurement Head said, raising his hand. All his colleagues burst out laughing seeing this. "Very good, Mathew. You will get a star if you answer this correctly," Chandra teased him.

Mathew sheepishly pulled his hand down and said, "Identify the biggest rock and crush it to reduce its size."

"Wonderful," said TOC Guru. "But, how do you identify the biggest rock in our river, Mr. Mathew?" continuing with his questions.

There was a moment of silence as the group pondered over this. "Might sound absurd, but here is my thought. Reduce the level of water, and the biggest rock will pop out first on its own," Mathew added tentatively.

"Fantastic, Mr. Mathew. And, I think you know what my next question is going to be. How will you reduce our level of water in production so that the biggest obstacle to achieving flow pops up on its own? Meaning, how will the CCR pop up on its own?"

Ganapatiji groaned in despair. "TOC Guru, what all problems will you make us solve, eh?" but he continued thinking about the question. TOC Guru took the opportunity to refill his coffee mug and came back to his seat, stirring his coffee.

"Aha, I got it," exclaimed Ganapatiji. "We should reduce the WIP so that the CCR emerges on its own, right?"

"Hold on," Chandra, the Sales Head jumped in. "If you reduce the WIP, the output will come down drastically due to starvation of work across the resources, is it not?"

"Absolutely," TOC Guru said with a smile toward Abhinav. "And, that is not something any Sales Head would appreciate. And, with good reason. Just as very high WIP is a problem, very low WIP is also a concern. We can't risk that happening."

"Then, what does that mean? The middle path, eh? Neither too high nor too low, but a sort of medium WIP. Is that fine?" Ganapatiji asked everyone around the room.

"You are on fire today, Ganapatiji," TOC Guru said excitedly. "That is a great starting point if we are to identify the CCR in order to improve the flow."

And, although everyone expected him to throw another question at them, he simply kept quiet, pretending to be quite taken up with something in his coffee mug. Abhinav chuckled to himself. "Now, he won't even give them the correct questions. They will have to come up with that themselves."

There was a minute of silence as the group wondered what was going to happen next. TOC Guru did not seem to be in any hurry, nor uncomfortable with the silence in the room. He merrily continued to sip his coffee.

"Er,..." Mathew cleared his throat and decided to break the silence. "Ok, so, the WIP has to be neither too high nor too low; but how do we reduce the current WIP to the medium level? And what exactly is this medium level? Anyone clear on this?" he asked, looking around at his colleagues. Naresh was thinking hard. He got up and walked toward the whiteboard and started writing down some numbers. "See, our current WIP on the shop floor is 75 days from start to end. The question is, how do we bring it down to the medium level? That is, say, approximately 35 to 40 days?" "Do we do that by parking the excess 35 to 40 days of WIP outside the production floor?" Sanjay asked, not looking very confident. There were laughs around the room. "Sanjay, Sir, it is not such a simple and straightforward answer. There are commitments that we have made to our customers, and if we park some of the orders that are in WIP outside, what will happen to those date commitments? Especially with the current experience of long lead times, even if we keep it inside the WIP queue, we are not sure that we would be able to honor those, and you are suggesting that we take them completely out of the queue? I will tell you what will happen - lead times are going to increase further, and we will have a bunch of very angry customers calling us day and night," Chandra, the Sales Head, did not look amused at all at the direction the discussion was moving toward.

Naresh tried to placate his irked colleague. "Calm down, Chandra. We are just exploring the possibilities here, aren't we? I do understand your concern, but the reduction in WIP should increase the flow and hence reduce the lead times, isn't it?" he said, pointing toward the results summarized by Abhinav on the whiteboard post the second scenario of the dice game that they had played the previous day.

"Great point, Nareshji," with a booming voice, Ganapatiji joined the conversation. "Taking out the WIP outside means we can quarantine them in the shop floor itself, so that it does not clutter the flow."

As soon as he finished saying this, however, Ganapatiji looked a bit perplexed. "But the next question is - which WIP, meaning orders, should we quarantine, and which ones should we continue to work on? Is there a way to smartly determine this? I don't know!"

"That is all very well. But whatever be the answer, I do not want cascading failures on our date commitments to our customers. I can't even imagine the repercussions," Chandra said with a warning note.

Again, there was silence in the room. And TOC Guru didn't do anything to help them out, noted Abhinav. "This is what I need to master – not get flustered by the many awkward silences."

"Why don't we take up what our Sales Head here is warning us about as the starting point? Meaning, let us sort the current WIP in descending order of our date commitment. And we do that to our full order list. If we want to allow approximately 40 days' worth of WIP into the system, that means we subtract 40 days from the committed due date. All orders outside this will be quarantined. What do you say?" Naresh tried to bring some clarity to the discussion.

"That is a great way to decide what we should process and what we should quarantine," Ganapatiji latched onto that suggestion and immediately opened an Excel sheet on his laptop to see how that suggestion looked when applied to the current order book.

"Out of a total of 94 orders - which adds up to 75 days of load - when due date commitments are sorted in descending order, and when we subtract 40 from the committed due dates, 50 orders are qualified to be in the WIP. The rest, that is, 44 orders have to wait outside to enter the WIP," he announced to the whole team.

"Excellent, Ganapatiji," Naresh chimed. "What this means is that we have correctly identified 50 orders as the active orders in WIP, while the rest of the orders are waiting in WIP."

Everyone looked excited at the progress made. But Chandra, the Sales Head, still looked unconvinced. "That is all very well. My question is - when will you release those WIP from waiting to active?"

"Logically speaking that should be when it is 40 days from the due date, isn't it? That is when it gets an entry ticket to the WIP queue, I think. Let us consider this with an actual scenario," and here, Ganapatiji picked up a random work order from his Excel. "Look at this order that has its due date as 15th Dec. Now, if you subtract 40 days from that date, you get the date as 06th Nov. On that day, this work order gets an entry ticket to enter the active WIP queue." The others nodded in agreement. The picture seemed to be emerging slowly, steadily, and clearly.

Everyone turned to look at Chandra to see if he was also convinced. Chandra was peering into the Excel and did not look all that excited.

"What about these orders then?" he asked, pointing toward a few rows in Ganapatiji's Excel. "There are roughly 12 or 15 orders that are already past our committed dates. Surely, we cannot just neglect them?"

"Of course not," Mathew jumped in. "What this means is that these orders should be our top priority. Better late than never, as the saying goes!" Chandra nodded in agreement.

"That does sound logical," Naresh added, but he did not sound totally convinced. "But isn't that going to be risky for us? What if, in the process of expediting these delayed orders, we put those orders that are just 40 days before the due date into jeopardy? We may continue to play catch up and never be ahead of the game!"

"True, and I have another parameter to add to this, sorry," Sanjay, the Finance Head, interrupted Naresh. Timeline is just one factor, an important one, I agree, but definitely not the only criteria for us to determine which work orders get into the WIP queue and which get quarantined. These orders," and here he pointed at a few line items in the Excel, "well, they are not past their due dates, and nor have they crossed significant production processes, but have very high margins for us. Shouldn't they be taken up on priority? We can at least offset a few losses by doing this."

There were many nods around the table, and it led to many small discussions within the room. Confusion was written large across the faces of almost everyone in the room. Each one began to suggest which orders should be given top priority. Then, Ganapatiji interrupted all of them. "Gentlemen, let me try and clarify this with something that happened to me while I was in college." Everyone stopped speaking and began to listen to what Ganapatiji had to say. "During my third year of college, a couple of my close friends and I decided to go on a road trip to Ooty from Coimbatore. Yuvraj and Ramanathan had never been to Ooty and were very excited. This was a long weekend, I remember. And, so, we set out on a Friday evening with our bags and maps. Remember, no GPS those days?"

"Were there roads back then, Ganapatiji?" Chandra's question was met with laughter from everyone in the room, except Ganapatiji, who decided to ignore this query. He continued with his story. "Unfortunately, it seemed as if quite a few others had a similar idea for the long weekend. The traffic was unbelievable. The fact that it was terribly hot in Coimbatore might have been another factor for this mass exodus to cooler Ooty. Anyway, the upshot of it all was that we had to crawl our way forward. The fact that Rama was not that familiar with driving on hilly roads, and since it started pouring heavily very soon after we started our journey, meant that the drive was far from being a pleasant experience."

Here Ganapatiji paused to sip some water and then continued.

"To make matters really, really worse, though, we met with an accident. And, boy, quite a serious one. Rama had no idea that a truck was coming out of a side road at great speed. I still remember the sickening thud of metal on metal, and it seemed as if the whole of my insides were going to come out through my mouth. The car turned turtle and slid along the wet road for what seemed like an eternity, but in truth might have been just a few seconds. Fortunately, nothing happened to any of us. In fact, since I had fastened my seat belt even though I was sitting in the rear seat, I came out relatively unscathed. Rama got injured the most, and there was blood all over him. There was a deep gash on his head. We had to check his pulse to make sure that he was not dead. Yuvraj was also in a bad shape. His hand was severely twisted, and we suspected that it was broken. I was dazed and had a few cuts here and there, but was fine otherwise. Nothing had happened to the truck or its passengers, of course. But, fortunately for us, they did not simply drive away but came to our rescue. A few locals also came out quickly. We were somehow extricated from the mangled mess of a car, and an improvised stretcher was made to carry us to a nearby hospital. I was able to hobble across to a nearby shop and make a few phone calls to our families. My thought was I should let them know that even though we were in an accident, we were fine, and that we were on our way to a nearby hospital. My idea was also to seek their help if we needed to go to a different doctor or hospital for whatever reason."

Ganapatiji looked around to see that everyone was paying attention to his college adventures. He continued.

"Obviously, now I realize what a mistake it was – calling our parents. They didn't get reassured at all that we were in safe hands. They somehow managed to find the number of that small hospital and insisted on speaking to the doctor personally to make sure that we received the right treatment at the earliest possible time. And, although, I can understand their mental framework at that time, I am really not proud of what happened next. From the doctor, I came to know that all our parents began to insist that he treats their child first. He was visibly annoyed while narrating this, and I felt quite sheepish myself. To make matters worse, the parents began to pull rank with the young, hapless doctor, it seems. My dad made sure to let the doctor know that he was a local district secretary of our current ruling party in the state, Yuvraj's mother held a very senior position in the Collector's office, and Ramanathan's father was a very well-known businessman in Chennai. And, it was his car that we were driving, and which was now a total mess."

The others nodded in understanding.

Ganapatiji paused again to have a sip of water. He then looked around at the attentive faces around him and gave a loud laugh. "Of course, we managed to come out of that accident without loss of life or limb, although, Rama still walks with a slight limp."

"Was wondering if you survived that crash, Ganapatiji," Sanjay said with a straight face. The others laughed on hearing this.

"While all this is very interesting, Ganapatiji, why are you telling us your wild teenage adventures when we are trying to solve our company's numerous challenges?" wondered Mathew.

"Aah, the point I was trying to make was this. With multiple phone calls from our parents, putting pressure on the young doctor to attend to their son, I was reminded of the situation we were discussing a while back. The young doctor must have experienced severe stress. On top of the stress he might have felt in terms of the line of treatment he should adopt to make sure that we came out of the incident with minimal to no serious impact, isn't it?" Ganapatiji outlined why he suddenly got reminded this incident from his past.

"I still don't get it, Ganapatiji," said Mathew. "What point in our discussion are you referring to here?"

"Mathewji, I am, of course, referring to the question about which order to process first," Ganapatiji looked a bit annoyed.

"Aah, ok, now I get it. All 3 of you were work orders for the doctor, right!" Mathew said with a laugh.

Ganapatiji ignored this remark and continued. "I remember I was quite impressed by the way the young doctor responded to these calls. How he went about his job. While we were sipping tea after he had completed attending to all 3 of us, I apologized on behalf of all the parents. He smiled and brushed it aside. 'I can understand their concern, of course. Besides, they are not even here, and so have no idea who got injured the most, etc. I am sure if they were present, all would have agreed that the young man with spectacles was the one most in danger,' he said referring to Ramanathan. 'I still remember his simple manner and gentle ways. My job is to save my patient's life. Every one of them. And, if I see 2 or 3 seriously injured ones coming into the clinic, I have to make a few quick decisions. I have to quickly surmise who is most badly injured, and in a critical state. Unfortunately, I am the only doctor here. There are a couple of nurses to assist me. I cannot expect them to handle critical cases, of course.

"So, he prioritized Ramanathan as he was injured the most. Thereafter, he focused on Yuvraj and finally you," said Sanjay.

"Precisely. And, within a few days even Rama was fit to travel, and so we returned to Coimbatore," said Ganapatiji.

"Quite an interesting story, Ganapatiji. What this means is that we should identify who our Rama, Yuvraj, and Ganapatiji are from among those orders that are already released in active WIP, so that we don't confuse the doctor with multiple priorities," Naresh brought the story back to the topic under discussion. "But, who is the doctor here?" he asked, looking a bit perplexed.

"Isn't that obvious, Naresh? It is the worker who is acting on the WIP. And, his objective should be to save the order's life, meaning completing it on time," Mathew interjected.

"I understood that, Mathew," Naresh replied. "But my question is how does the worker figure out which order is in a critical state and which one is not?"

"The story of the doctor with 3 patients is good, and it is good and relatively easy to prioritize whom to focus on. But, in our case, we deal with 40 to 50 orders at any point in time, isn't it? Before taking up the order for work, it will be tremendously difficult for our workers to meticulously calculate which order is in which category," Chandra chipped in. Everyone nodded as soon as he finished speaking.

There was total silence in the room, except for the sound of TOC Guru moving his chair to get up and help himself to yet another cup of coffee. He did not seem to be in any hurry, nor did he look like he was keen to say anything at this point in time.

After a few more seconds of silence, Sanjay, the Finance Head, cleared his throat. Everyone looked in his direction eagerly. "For quite some time, I have been observing the simplicity of a mechanism that we use the world over to communicate flow priority to the masses, irrespective of their educational or intellectual background or capabilities. Do you folks know what I am referring to here?" he asked, looking around, but was met with blank faces. "It is very familiar to all of us. We see at least 3 or 4 of them on any given day, and get frustrated by it; but in case it is not working properly, we are in deep, deep trouble. Still no idea what I am talking about?" he looked around, clearly enjoying himself.

"A traffic signal," Ganapatiji almost shouted his answer, looking very pleased with himself.

"Of course, you would get the answer to that question, Ganapatiji," said Mathew with a laugh. "Have you paid the fine, by the way, for getting fined for crossing that red signal at Valsad?" The others joined in the laughter. Ganapatiji looked a bit sheepish but kept quiet.

"Thanks to Ganapatiji breaking traffic rules, we may have stumbled upon a way out of our current challenge. Can't we use something similar for our workers to identify which work order is Yuvraj, which one is Rama, etc.?" Sanjay continued. "The most critical will be red, and the least critical one would be green." He went to the whiteboard and wrote this down.

"Hey, it suddenly strikes me," said Mathew. "Your accident, Ganapatiji, on your way to Ooty. The doctor, in fact, followed the traffic light code, didn't he? Treated Rama first — R for Red; followed by Yuvraj — Y for Yellow, and finally you, Ganapatiji — G for Green."

"Fantastic!" cried TOC Guru. "Brilliant, in fact. But, I doubt if Ganapatiji's friends called him Ganapati-ji back then; but then I won't be really surprised even if they did!" Everyone laughed heartily on hearing this, nodding their heads in agreement.

TOC Guru continued when they all settled down again, "Am super excited that you folks thought of this all on your own. I have been observing the conversations for a while, and am really happy to see all you pitching in and solving all this on your own. Great going. This coloring system is a simple but highly effective mechanism to know the right priority of the many orders in the work in progress."

"That is all very good, TOC Guru. But what about those orders that have already lost their lives? Meaning, orders whose due dates have already passed?" Ganapatiji asked.

"Hmm, good point; but I think the solution is quite simple. We add one more color to our traffic light. Universally, the color black represents anything sad, negative, etc. We can use the same," Sanjay quickly replied and added that to the board.

"Let me get this straight. So, what you are saying is our priority will be – black, followed by red, and then yellow, and, finally, green, right? I meant, decreasing order of priority, of course," Ganapatiji wanted to ensure that there was no ambiguity regarding this.

"Bang on," Chandra, the Sales Head jumped in to the discussion. "If we follow this, I will feel confident that every order is getting the right and impartial treatment it deserves with respect to our due date commitments."

"Fantastic. The picture of how we can manage the operations is getting clearer," said Ganapatiji, but he did not look all that happy.

"What now, Ganapatiji?" asked Sanjay. "I know you are going to add a 'but' to your statement. Let us all hear it," Sanjay said.

"Yes, you are right. All this is looking fine, but one point is still bothering me. "How and where do I find myself?" Ganapatiji asked, looking confused.

"Eh, now, what is this, Ganapatiji?" asked Mathew, looking bewildered. "Are you also a religious or a spiritual Guru, TOC Guru?" he asked, turning to face TOC Guru.

"Of course not, Mathewji. That is not what I meant to ask," Ganapatiji quickly clarified. "What I meant was – how and where do we find the CCR, the role I played in the dice simulation games."

That brought clarity to the rest of the audience.

"Now, that is an interesting question," TOC Guru stepped in to answer that query from Ganapatiji. "With WIP reduced by almost half (since the number of orders will come down from the current 76 to active WIP of around 40, the waiting WIP will be close to 36), the level of water from our river example would now be almost half, isn't it?" The others were listening attentively and nodded in agreement.

"Good. Now, where do you think the water flow will slow down?" asked TOC Guru.

"Obviously ahead of the biggest obstacle to the flow – meaning ahead of the resource that has the lowest capacity," Mathew, the Procurement Head answered.

"Good, now what is that resource called?" TOC Guru continued to ply them with questions.

"Capacity Constraint Resource, CCR," Ganapatiji seemed a little irritated at being asked these basic questions! But Sanjay quickly jumped in with another question.

"All of us have understood about the concept of the CCR, TOC Guru; but the role I played - as the RM release resource number 1, I have a question around that. We changed our operating paradigm from dice scenario 1 to scenario 2, didn't we? Abhinav did not give me any dice during scenario 2. However, I was asked to release WIP in line with the output of CCR. How does that fall in place here? What is the significance of that variation that you brought in to the game? I am unable to piece that with the rest of our discussion," Sanjay looked clearly confused but seemed unable to articulate his question in a better manner.

"How are RM releases controlled as per CCR output – that is what you intended to ask, right, Sanjayji?" Ganapatiji clarified the same with shopfloor lingo. And then he continued on a different but related train of thought. "Hmm, this also means that we cannot continue to release our work orders as per the due date – 40 criteria that we discussed earlier, isn't it?" he asked referring to the earlier discussion on the entry ticket for work orders into the active WIP queue.

"Absolutely brilliant," TOC Guru appreciated this line of thinking. "Yes, now releases should be in tune with CCR output, as we understood from scenario 2 of our dice game."

"Understood TOC Guru. If we release more work orders into the active WIP queue than the CCR output, then WIP will pile up, and lead time will go high. And if we release lesser than the CCR output, then CCR will starve, and overall output will come down," Sanjay asserted.

"That is fine, and all of us have understood how we should release work orders from the waiting bucket into the active WIP queue. My question is different. What about future orders? These would need to be added to the waiting bucket, isn't it?" Naresh asked pointedly.

"What about it – should be the same way, isn't it?" Ganapatiji reacted quickly.

"Wait a minute, Ganapatiji. That may not be the case," Chandra, the Sales Head stepped in. "And that is because we give due date commitment to our customers based on standard lead times. This means there is an assumption that the release dates are also standard. However, when we release orders from the waiting bucket based on CCR output – I see some disconnect here, but am not sure what exactly!"

"Excellent point, Mr. Chandra," TOC Guru said in a booming voice. "The real question should be, should we continue to quote due dates based on the standard lead times?"

Sanjay replied, "I don't think so. I believe the way we triggered the release dates into active WIP, the due dates should also be quoted in accordance with the CCR. CCR appears to be the ultimate flow controller."

"Fantastic point, Sanjayji," TOC Guru shouted in excitement and loudly clapped his hands to show how much he appreciated this insight from the Finance Head.

"Yes! Now that the WIP flow is almost balanced in tune with the CCR, when do you want the new order to be worked on by the CCR, if we want to adhere to the due date commitment?" The group took a minute to digest this rather long-winded question from TOC Guru.

"I am not really sure I understood your question; but are you asking which is the safest due date between the 4 traffic color zones?" Sanjay asked very tentatively referring to his earlier traffic lights example.

"Yes, yes," said Ganapatiji impatiently on behalf of TOC Guru. "And the answer to that is obviously yellow. And that is because if any problem happens to the flow of this order, post CCR, we can recover its life before its death, meaning we will avert it from going into the black zone."

"Fantastic, Ganapatiji. And now, please tell us the answer to this next question: Where is this yellow zone available in the priority?" TOC Guru threw another question at the group.

"In the middle, obviously. Between the red and green priority zones," Ganapatiji replied immediately.

"Good. If we want the new order to be worked by CCR in the safe zone - which is yellow - what should be the due date?" TOC Guru probed further.

Now, this was a tough query for the group. Even after some 5 to 10 minutes of thinking, no one ventured to come up with an answer. Seeing this, TOC Guru went to the board and began to write something.

"Say, for example, today is the 1st December. Assume that the CCR has active WIP till 5th Jan. When do you think the CCR can work on a new order?" he asked.

"Obviously on 6th Jan," Ganapatiji answered.

"Hold on," interjected Naresh. "What happens to the orders in the waiting bucket?"

"Excellent question, Naresh," said TOC Guru nodding approvingly at the direction of Naresh. "Let us say, there are 15 days' worth of orders waiting in the waiting bucket. Now tell me."

Naresh did some quick calculation and said, "That will be the 16th from 5th Jan. Meaning 22nd Jan."

"So far so good. And now, if we want this 22nd Jan date as the yellow zone for the new order, what should be its due date?" TOC Guru gently led the team in the right direction.

"Assuming that the yellow zone is the middle, it should be the WIP limit of 40 divided by 2?" Naresh asked with a hint of uncertainty in his voice.

"Of course. Meaning, 20 days from 22nd Jan, meaning, 11th Feb," cried TOC Guru, looking at the whole group to see if all of them were following his explanation.

"And that leads me to the conclusion that the ticket for this new order to enter into the active WIP should be 11th Feb – 40, meaning 2nd Jan," Ganapatiji said confidently.

"Superb," TOC Guru nodded approvingly at Ganapatiji.

There was silence in the room as the group took in all these considerations. After a while, Mathew asked with a tinge of sarcasm, "Today is the 1st Dec and the new work order will enter the active WIP queue on the 2nd Jan. What will this order do all that while, eh? Sleeping?"

TOC Guru looked expectantly at Ganapatiji to see if he could counter this question from the Procurement Head. And sure enough, Ganapatiji seemed up to the task. "Good question, but I think I can take an analogy from a hospital or a nursing home."

But before he could continue, Sanjay interrupted Ganapatiji with a loud groan. "Come on, Ganapatiji. We all know that your elder daughter has managed to get a seat for an MBBS program in our most prestigious institute; but does that mean that you have become half a doctor yourself, and that too so quickly? All your examples are related to this profession all of a sudden!"

Everyone laughed at hearing this, including Ganapatiji. "Hahaha, Sanjayji. What to do? These days that is the only hot topic in my home. But let me continue with this just this once. I think it is quite relevant to our discussion. I have observed, and

I am sure, all of you here in this room would also have, that in almost all good hospitals, when patients are waiting in queue to consult their doctor, the duty nurse or the junior doctors check their basic health parameters. Such as height, weight, blood pressure, body temperature, etc., and they document these details in a hospital file. In some cases, I have even noticed these nurses or junior doctors asking patients if they are allergic to any medicines, food items, etc."

He paused and looked around the room. The others nodded in agreement. Ganapatiji continued. "The reason they are doing this is obviously to reduce the time that the main doctor needs to spend time with the patient."

"Ah, I see where you are going with this," Mathew cut Ganapatiji short. "Are you suggesting that we can also measure the BP and temperature of our work orders?" he asked with a twinkle in his eye. There was laughter in the room.

"Why not?" Chandra joined the conversation. "We can note down some key information such as where to ship the orders, the agreed price, inspection requirements, if any, packaging requirements, any special types of raw materials, etc."

"Also, the availability of all the required raw materials, packing materials, etc.," Mathew added to the list.

"I am assuming that all of you are making this checklist based on your real experience?" TOC Guru asked with a smile. "Hard lessons, eh?"

"Precisely, TOC Guru. Lessons learned from previous mistakes. Costly ones at times. We are not too keen to repeat these mistakes, as you may have guessed," Sanjay said, putting his hand to his head.

"Learning from our mistakes is intelligence, while learning from others' mistakes is smartness," Abhinav said all of a sudden, making his presence felt with this rather well-known quote.

TOC Guru laughed, but added, "We call this as a full-kit checklist. Obviously, it has 2 categories:

1. Information full-kit. How our Sales Head, Mr. Chandra, has described it, and

2. Material full-kit. How Mr. Mathew, our Procurement Head has described it."

TOC Guru wrote this down on the whiteboard. The group contemplated this for a few seconds, and then Naresh added, "the orders that are waiting in the waiting bucket for their release appointment can be subjected to this full-kit checklist; and, from the bank of full-kit cleared orders, releases can happen as per the output rate of CCR!"

"That's good; but, even if we perform both these checks sincerely – meaning, in true letter and spirit – it does not mean that all the obstacles to the flow of these orders can be prevented 100%," Sanjay chipped in, as he was responsible for quality as well. "There could be other problems like quality rejection/ rectification, machine breakdown, operator unavailability, etc.

And sometimes, this may obstruct the flow and we may miss the due dates."

"The orders that are getting into the red zone - identify the reasons for the same. Classify them as major and minor reasons, and apply the Pareto principle. Work on 20% of the causes to solve 80% of the effects," Ganapatiji said in response to Sanjay's comment.

"Excellent. Giving quality lessons to the Quality Head? I am impressed, Ganapatiji," Mathew said laughing.

"All thanks to last week's quality tools training by HR," Ganapatiji said trying to look modest.

"Excellent point, Ganapatiji," TOC Guru said. "This is the process to be followed to ensure that we are continuously improving the flow. The Process Of Ongoing Improvement, or POOGI, as we call it."

"Not to forget CAPA, Corrective And Preventive Action to be applied on the root cause of the problems identified through Pareto analysis," Abhinav spouted some more jargon.

At this point, Naresh accidentally caught sight of his mobile and exclaimed loudly. "Oh god! It is almost half-past 2 now! Isn't anyone hungry?" he asked looking at everyone around the room.

"Aah, now that you mention it, yes. I am feeling quite famished," said Sanjay. "But that was a most interesting discussion that we had. No wonder none of us felt hungry!"

"Let's quickly get something to eat, and we can re-assemble in 45 minutes. Is that fine with all of you?" asked Naresh. Everyone nodded in agreement.

And it was at this moment that someone opened the conference room. Naresh turned to see who the newcomer was and let out a gasp of excitement. It was the CEO of their company, Mr. Ratnapratap Chatterjee. He seemed surprised to see many from his leadership team assembled in a conference room, and that too on a Sunday.

"Hello Naresh. I see you have quite a few of our colleagues in today. Care to elaborate on what you are doing on a Sunday?" he asked.

Naresh and all the others were caught by surprise, and it took Naresh a couple of seconds to recover. He quickly got up from his seat and said, "Sir, these are my friends – TOC Guru and Abhinav. We are discussing ways and means of improving production."

At this point, Sanjay pitched in, "Yes Sir. The idea is to not delay any of our orders."

"You mean, 100% on-time performance?" the CEO looked genuinely surprised. "Isn't that a bit unrealistic given our current track record? I know how many of our orders are already delayed, and all of you are assembled on a Sunday dreaming about 100% on-time delivery?"

"Sir, yes, Sir. That is true; but with POOGI and CAPA, we should be ..." Ganapatiji blustered nervously.

TOC Guru – FLOW model

"What, POOGI? Ganapatiji, I am quite curious now. But, have you folks had lunch? If not, why don't we do that and after that you can explain what you plan to do?" asked the CEO with a smile.

"Sure, Sir, yes Sir," said Ganapatiji gratefully.

With that, everyone started moving out of the conference room and toward the cafeteria.

The CEO asked Naresh on the way out, "Did I hear you correctly? Your friend there is called TOC Guru? Surely that does not stand for Table of Contents?" he asked with a chuckle but did not wait for an answer and strode forward quickly.

Post lunch, Naresh opened his laptop and displayed the summary slide he had made over the past 2 days.

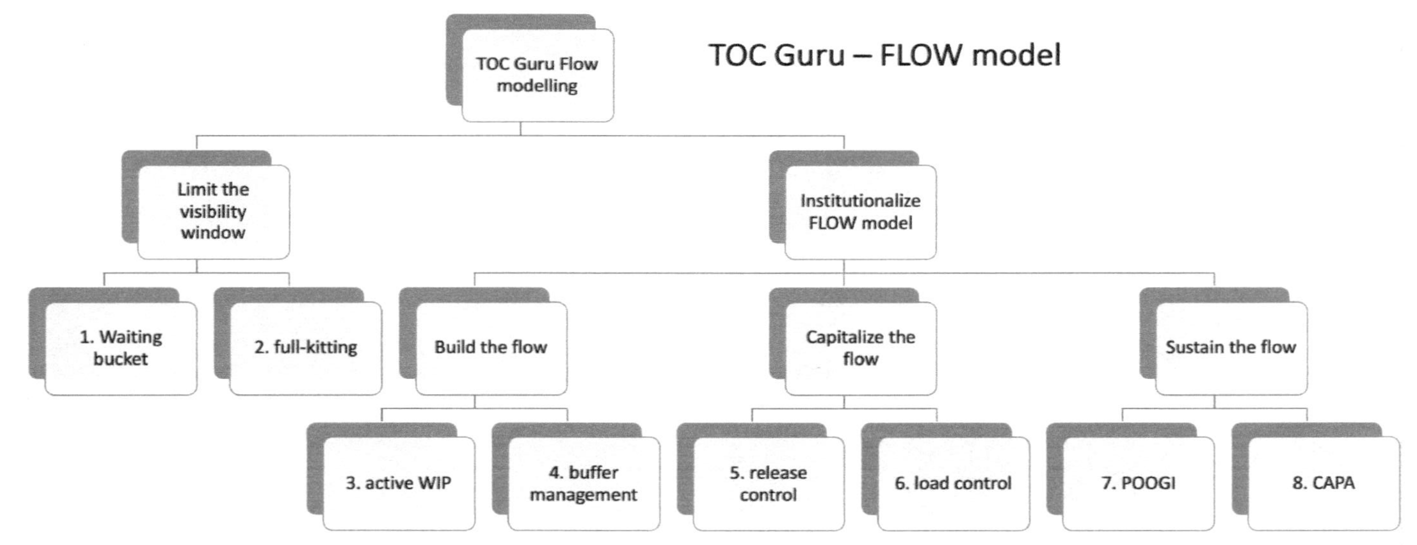

TOC Guru – FLOW model
TOC Guru Flow modelling
Limit the visibility window
Institutionalize FLOW model
1. Waiting bucket
2. full-kitting
Build the flow
Capitalize the flow
Sustain the flow
3. active WIP
4. buffer management
5. release control
6. load control
7. POOGI
8. CAPA

While explaining the blocks to the CEO, he also recapped the discussion for the audience. From time to time, TOC Guru also added some additional clarifications to make things clearer to the CEO. At the end of 30 minutes, there was a sigh of relief on the face of the CEO. "This makes a lot of sense. What I gather is you first de-clutter the shop floor so that orders flow better, and then onwards..." But Ganapatiji was not listening. He was mesmerized by the charm of the CEO and his American accent. "No wonder he graduated from one of the premier management institutes in America. Youngest CEO of a textile company!" Meanwhile, Mr. Ratnapratap Chatterjee continued, "Why don't we try from tomorrow? You can name this intervention 'De-clutter to FLOW better' with Naresh being the Project Head?" "Fantastic, Sir," all shouted in excitement. Naresh looked quite pleased. Having received the blessings of the CEO, the team was doubly elated. They were raring to implement the new learnings from the very next day.

Chapter 15

Wed Together

It was a Wednesday morning, and Abhinav was free for a while from back-to-back meetings for a short period of time. A week had gone by since their marathon meeting with Naresh and his team at the Pioneer Mills premises. He stepped away from his workstation and started moving toward the coffee machine when he caught sight of TOC Guru rushing somewhere. But as soon as he caught sight of Abhinav, TOC Guru slowed down, and they exchanged some pleasantries.

"But where are you rushing like this?" asked Abhinav.

"To meet HR. Have to travel now that Covid restrictions are no longer in place, Abhinav."

"Oh, nice. Where to this time? Somewhere nice and exotic?" asked Abhinav with a twinkle in his eyes.

"Indonesia. Now, I don't think that qualifies as 'exotic' according to me. Not sure what you think about it. For 3 months. At least that is what I think it will be, as of now. You remember that transformation project?" said TOC Guru.

"Oh, great. Congratulations. So, that means we got that multi-million dollar project, right? You were very keen to bag that one, I remember," said Abhinav warmly, shaking TOC Guru's hand.

"Oh yes, finally. There were so many back-and-forth emails, numerous meetings, that I thought we may not get it. But, thankfully, my fears proved to be unfounded. This will be a big plus for our organization, Abhinav," replied TOC Guru with a bit smile on his face.

"But, tell me. What is happening with Naresh and Ganapatiji?" TOC Guru suddenly recalled.

"Oh, I was about to update you on that but was not sure if you had the time. But, let me quickly bring you up to date on that one. Naresh and I are in regular touch. The team started in earnest the very next day, that is, Monday. They first cleaned up their current order book by removing dubious entries and unclosed orders whose deliveries had already been completed in the past. Then, they reconciled the committed due dates on the cleaned order book after holding discussions with the customers, especially of those whose due dates are in the past. And, as a result of that, from the order book of 106, they brought down the work orders to 95. Their current WIP was approximately 70 days. After much deliberation, they considered 47 orders as active WIP, and the WIP was brought down to 40 days. The remaining 48 orders were put in the quarantine list, parked, and waiting to join the WIP queue."

"Great! So far, so good," TOC Guru nodded in approval. "They are moving in the right direction. They are a smart lot and can now easily implement the flow model that we discussed with them last weekend." He caught sight of his watch and said suddenly, "Oh god. I really need to rush now. Lots pending before I can say I am ready to board the flight! But do give me a heads up from time to time, will you? And pull me in for any discussion if you feel my intervention is required, ok?" He was already walking toward the HR area. Abhinav did not try to detain him but nodded in agreement and wished him luck in Indonesia. Although he knew that Naresh and his team were smart and capable, he was relieved to hear TOC Guru offering his time and expertise. "They will need it. I will need it too," he thought to himself as he walked toward the coffee machine.

The weeks rolled by. Abhinav continued to be in regular touch with Naresh and his team. He even paid another visit to Pioneer Mills when he felt that it was important for him to be physically there to assist the team. They made good progress, but as anticipated, at some point, all of them were stuck. TOC Guru was true to his word. He happily joined them from Indonesia through Zoom and clarified a few concepts and recommended some strategies for the team. The team stumbled at times, but no one even thought of giving up. The first 2 weeks were really torturous, but later the implementation became a lot smoother. Results began to show, and that further motivated the team to go further.

"It's good to hear Naresh laughing. God, I was beginning to wonder if I had lost my best friend," Abhinav thought to himself. He was waiting to receive TOC Guru back in the office. The 3 months had flown by in a whirl. Exactly at 9:30 a.m., he caught sight of his mentor.

"Selamat Datang, TOC Guru," Abhinav welcomed him with a big smile on his face.

"Terima Kasih, Terima Kasih," TOC Guru responded.

"When did you reach India?" asked Abhinav.

"Last Friday. And, as you can guess, I immediately dashed off to my farm. And, here I am ready to wage yet another battle," TOC Guru replied with a laugh. "And, how are you? How is everything going? And, most importantly, how is Naresh?"

"All good. I spoke to him just last evening. They have improved a lot in their production management in the last 3 months. Their WIP has now gone down by half, their lead time has reduced by about 40%, and their output has increased by 25%. And, their on-time performance has skyrocketed to an incredible 90+%, TOC Guru!" exclaimed Abhinav delightedly.

"Wow. That is fantastic," exclaimed TOC Guru. "They have proved that they are smart and unconventional thinkers and executors," he added generously letting them take all the credit. "This should definitely have had a positive impact on their business then, isn't it?"

"Absolutely, TOC Guru. All thanks to your expert recommendations. Now, their order book is full, as their customers are delighted with their delivery performance. What is more? The customers don't even bother to negotiate with them on the price. Pioneer Mills is not compromising on their margin through negotiations as they used to do earlier!"

"Excellent. That means the impact is on both fronts - top line with a higher order book, and bottom line with better margin realization," TOC Guru said. And, after a pause, he added, "Very happy to hear the news. This should be a great relief to your friend Naresh, isn't it?"

"Yes, absolutely. In fact, he told me just yesterday that he is being considered for the newly created post of the Chief Operating Officer (COO) within his company to manage the rest of the plants under their group," Abhinav said excitedly.

"The news keeps getting better and better," TOC Guru said, looking very happy. He paused for a second and then asked, "I'm really, really happy for your friend, Abhinav. May he get more success professionally; but what about his personal front? You hinted at some challenges there, with his girlfriend? I mean, we obviously did not discuss that in great detail. But, I do remember hearing you say that since he hardly got any quality time to spend with her, their relationship had hit a rough patch."

"Exactly. Though I won't blame Priya either. She has been the epitome of patience and understanding. Any other girl would have walked out years ago. Not that I am blaming my friend either. This is one of those situations where neither party is to be blamed, as you can imagine. But, I am really, really glad to tell you that they have managed to turn things around, TOC Guru. His professional success has had a huge positive impact on his personal life. So much so that now they are thinking of taking the next step. Naresh has proposed marriage to Priya, in fact. Seems she was really shocked and almost spilled her cup of coffee when he brought the topic up." Seeing the look of concern on TOC Guru's face, Abhinav quickly added, "When I said 'shocked,' I meant 'pleasantly shocked,' of course. She said 'yes' and the wedding is slated to happen in 6 months' time, I think. Both their families are delighted, and, I suspect, a bit relieved as well!"

"Wow! That is fantastic news, indeed," TOC Guru said excitedly, clapping Abhinav on his back.

"But, you will have a bigger surprise soon, TOC Guru," Abhinav said with a mischievous grin.

And, at that moment, as if on cue, Naresh and Priya entered the meeting room. There was no mistaking what was in Naresh's hand – a fancy wedding invitation card along with a big box of sweets. Ignoring the hand that Naresh offered, TOC Guru gave a big hug to Naresh. Naresh then introduced Priya to TOC Guru, saying, "Priya, this is the man responsible for the smile you see on my face!" And, when Priya looked quizzically at him, he added, "Apart from you, of course!" TOC Guru and Abhinav laughed on hearing this. "Quick thinking, my friend," said TOC Guru. He warmly greeted Priya and asked her a few details about herself, the marriage, etc.

But, Naresh wasn't done thanking TOC Guru. "Priya, on a serious note, it is all thanks to TOC Guru that I have managed to stabilize my professional turbulence and the resultant personal turbulence!"

Priya smiled and said, "Yes, you may have mentioned this one or 2 times," and turning toward TOC Guru and Abhinav, she added, "Flow, that is all he has been talking about. The importance of maintaining flow! I suspect he is trying to implement his new learnings while planning for the wedding as well!"

TOC Guru and Abhinav laughed out loud, while Naresh looked a bit sheepish.

Priya then said, "Thank you, TOC Guru, for all your help, and for returning the old Naresh to me. And, here is our wedding invitation. You are the first person to receive this. Naresh insisted that it has to be you, and I had no hesitation in agreeing with him on this!"

"Ah, you 2 youngsters in love. How wonderful to be so young and in love. And, what an absolute honor to be receiving this card from you both. I will, of course, be there with my better half."

"Just make sure there is excellent coffee. And, by the truckload," added Abhinav.

The 4 of them laughed and stepped out of the room.

The End